ISRAEL IN EGYPT

STUDIES IN BIBLICAL THEOLOGY

A series of monographs designed to provide the best work in biblical scholarship both in this country and abroad

Advisory Editors:

STUDIES IN BIBLICAL THEOLOGY

Second Series · 27

ISRAEL IN EGYPT

SIEGFRIED HERRMANN

SCM PRESS LTD
BLOOMSBURY STREET LONDON

Translated by Margaret Kohl from the German
Israels Aufenthalt in Ägypten,
Stuttgarter Bibelstudien 40, published 1970
by Verlag Katholisches Bibelwerk, Stuttgart

334 00739 9
First British Edition 1973
Published by SCM Press Ltd
56 Bloomsbury Street London

Printed in Great Britain by
W & J Mackay Limited, Chatham

FOR
MARIA MAGDALENA
AND
MATTHIAS-MARCUS

CONTENTS

INTRODUCTION

'Israel in Egypt' is a subject of unique fascination. It has been a time-honoured theme down to our own day, and has occupied and inspired students of the past no less than musicians and painters, writers and film producers. We have only to think of Handel's oratorio *Israel in Egypt*;[1] of Thomas Mann's tetralogy *Joseph and his Brethren*;[2] of interpretations in painting and sculpture, where the story of Moses has been a particularly favourite theme;[3] or of the film epic's fanciful and fantastic attempts to capture Moses and the Israelites on the wide screen and to bring alive their ancient story. Parallel to all these are the endeavours of scholars, especially Egyptologists and the theologians concerned with the history of the Old Testament; these continue down to the present day and are so numerous and so varying in range that it would need a separate scholarly study to do them justice.[4]

The concern of such different disciplines with this outstanding subject allows us almost to forget that it is in essence exclusively a biblical theme; that it is biblical figures and destinies which have had this stimulating and fruitful effect. The secret of the fascination which we touched on at the beginning is precisely the fact that here biblical material has direct contact with world history, with a history in which the Israelites, the 'people of God' (though yet hardly perceptible as an entity), stood in living contact with a great power, a power whose dominant religious and cultural role was, and is, undisputed, and whose after-effects influenced and helped to form the European consciousness in many different ways. This great power was ancient Egypt,[5] Egypt in the declining phase of what is known as the New Kingdom, which under the Ramessids enjoyed a last real zenith of independent greatness. It was a unique historical constellation which brought young Israel, at this moment of its earliest history, into contact with such influential power, even if at the same time it parted company from Egypt in dramatic circumstances to take up its own self-sufficient and independent course, a course which in turn made world history. As a result, this constellation challenges both scholars and amateurs in all the areas of culture involved in the events which comprise it. Theologians and Egyptologists are asked professionally about the meaning and effects of the course of events which we call Israel's sojourn in Egypt; they are asked about the historical circumstances and the effects of that stay, testimony to which penetrated far and wide not only into the religious consciousness but even into the general historical consciousness of the world, exerting on both art and literature the influence that we have seen.

Interesting though it is, we shall not be pursuing this later history here. The purpose of the present study is rather to build up from the scattered information and testimony of biblical and non-biblical texts as reliable a picture as possible of the historical context in which what we know as Israel's sojourn in Egypt belonged; and to discover what ultimately small, local events they were which had such far-reaching effects. What seem at first sight to be independent and detailed accounts in the Book of Exodus turn out on closer examination to be highly complicated sources, composed of different elements and varying in value. Since, however, they are the only testimonies which give us a direct account of Israel's stay in Egypt, we are bound to make them our starting point; but at the same time we must see them in the wider context to which they belong, practically at the beginning of the Old Testament.

ABBREVIATIONS

ANEP	*The Ancient Near East in Pictures relating to the Old Testament*, ed. J. B. Pritchard
ANET	*Ancient Near Eastern Texts relating to the Old Testament*, ed. J. B. Pritchard
AO	Der Alte Orient
AOB	*Altorientalische Bilder zum Alten Testament*, ed. H. Gressmann
AOT	*Altorientalische Texte zum Alten Testament*, ed. H. Gressmann
ASAE	*Annales du Service des Antiquités de l'Égypte*
BASOR	*Bulletin of the American Schools of Oriental Research*
BWANT	Beiträge zur Wissenschaft vom Alten und Neuen Testament
BZAW	Beihefte zur *Zeitschrift für die alttestamentliche Wissenschaft*
CAH	*The Cambridge Ancient History*
EvTh	*Evangelische Theologie*
FRLANT	Forschungen zur Religion und Literatur des Alten und Neuen Testaments
JBL	*Journal of Biblical Literature*
JEA	*Journal of Egyptian Archaeology*
JNES	*Journal of Near Eastern Studies*
JSS	*Journal of Semitic Studies*
KBL	L. Köhler – W. Baumgartner, *Lexicon in Veteris Testamenti libros*
KuD	*Kerygma und Dogma*
OTL	Old Testament Library
OTS	*Oudtestamentische Studiën*

RB	*Revue Biblique*
SBS	Stuttgarter Bibelstudien
SBT	Studies in Biblical Theology
SVT	Supplements to *Vetus Testamentum*
ThLZ	*Theologische Literaturzeitung*
TDNT	*Theological Dictionary of the New Testament*, ed. G. Kittel
ThZ	*Theologische Zeitschrift*
VT	*Vetus Testamentum*
WO	Die Welt des Orients
ZAW	*Zeitschrift für die alttestamentliche Wissenschaft*
ZDMG	*Zeitschrift der Deutschen Morgenländischen Gesellschaft*
ZDPV	*Zeitschrift des Deutschen Palästina-Vereins*
ZThK	*Zeitschrift für Theologie und Kirche*

I

THE BIBLICAL EVIDENCE

Israel's stay in Egypt is part of a great historical narrative, which is presented to the reader of the Bible almost without a break in the so-called Five Books of Moses, the Pentateuch. The patriarch Abraham obeys the call of his God and moves out of Mesopotamia[1] with his family into southern Palestine, where he gains a footing, settling down in the country round about Hebron. We are told that his son Isaac stayed with his herds still further south, in the Beersheba area, but was unable to gain any permanent influence from there. Isaac's second son Jacob, having bought the firstborn's blessing belonging to his brother Esau, seems to have been the first to be called to fulfil the promise which had already been made to Abraham – the promise of becoming a great nation, with land of its own. Jacob begets the twelve sons who were one day to be the progenitors of future Israel. But this came about by a curiously devious path, and at first not in Palestine at all. Joseph, the youngest but one of the twelve brothers, is sold into Egypt. There he succeeds, through particular circumstances, in rising to important offices in the state, and, since he was a far-sighted economic and political organizer, he manages to avert a famine, whose effects were apparently felt as far afield as Palestine. Because of this the sons of Jacob come to buy food in Egypt, not knowing that their brother Joseph holds the leading position in the Egyptian economic apparatus. In the familiar dramatic circumstances, Jacob and his sons meet Joseph again in Egypt, settle down there and gradually grow into a great people which alarms even the Egyptians. It is in the course of the Egyptian government's counter-measures against the further expansion of these people that the boy Moses is saved. Incidents between the Egyptians

and the 'Hebrews', in which Moses takes the 'Hebrew' part,
later force him to flee into the desert of the Sinai peninsula, where
he experiences a divine revelation and is given the task of leading
his people out of Egypt, after negotiations with the Pharaoh, the
Egyptian king. The Pharaoh's resistance to letting Moses and his
people go is broken by a series of fearful plagues. Moses and his
flock are able to leave the country. An Egyptian troop which
pursues them is exterminated at the Reed Sea – according to
another version is actually destroyed through miraculous divine
intervention. Thus the way is opened up for the emigrants to the
once-more promised goal of entering a land flowing with milk and
honey. One of the many incidents of the journey through the
desert is the great central event of early Israelite history: the encounter with the God of Mount Sinai, who through the mediation
of Moses proclaims law and justice to the awe-struck, waiting
people. After a considerable stay in the oasis of Kadesh, the main
body of the tribes, we are told, neared the cultivated lands of
Palestine by way of the Edomite and Moabite country south,
south-east and east of the Dead Sea. It was granted to Moses to
look over to the land west of the Jordan from the peak of Mount
Nebo, north-east of the Dead Sea – a land which he himself was
not destined to enter. He died before the very gates of the promised
land.

This is a finished historical narrative, even though it is admittedly
not moulded into one piece throughout, uniting in itself many
different forms of presentation. To understand it means entering
into the characteristic features of the oriental treatment of history
in general, and Old Testament history in particular. The historical
narrative of the Pentateuch is not reporting in the modern sense,
taking its bearings solely from the factual character of an event. It
is, rather, a pragmatic presentation of history; its intention is to
combine numerous individual units of historical tradition into a
convincing, self-contained, overall picture. It not only aims to lead
the reader along a chain of events; it also wants to make the
pattern of those events comprehensible to him. This means a
selection and ordering of the tradition: always in close contact
with what has been, but none the less under the guidance of overriding points of view; with emphases designed to promote the
understanding of the past, but primarily concerned to show the

individual's own present as being the final result of a purposeful development. History is not related for its own sake, but in order to justify a sense of continuity from which the people of Israel has drawn its greatest strength from time immemorial. It was God who, at the beginning of this history, called a single individual, Abraham, promising him that he would become a great people. This is the starting point of all further development. What was one day to be called Israel grew, over several generations, from the germ of a single patriarchal family. Whereas in the Book of Genesis the promise is still passed on from patriarch to patriarch, a first climax is reached through the multiplication of the patriarchal family in Egypt. The descendants of the patriarchs appear as an ethnic community, with a firm structure of its own, which is not abandoned by its God when its existence is threatened. Moses, as appointed witness of God, leads it out of the affliction into which it has fallen, afterwards mediating to the people divine law and justice for all time. The historical events appear step by step in the wake of a great historical process of revelation, which began with the patriarchs, continued in Egypt, and rose to classic heights in the work of Moses.

The concept which both ordered historical events in the interests of Israel's gradually developing history of faith and formed them into a single thread of salvation history, used the testimony of highly differing sources for its finished pattern. These sources can be shown to derive from different periods and areas of early Israelite history and they must be evaluated individually. What is offered to the historian in the Pentateuch is a pragmatically ordered collection of sources, each of whose individual components has its own considerable value. Form and content stand in close interrelationship to one another and still show clearly enough the circumstances – the original historical relationships and situations – which were their background and from which they emerged.

The most obvious difference between the traditions about the patriarchs in Genesis and the much more unified exodus tradition, from the Book of Exodus onwards, is that Genesis takes the form of a family history of the patriarchs; whereas in the Book of Exodus and beyond it, Israel is presupposed as a completed national whole, and its division into separate tribes and groups of tribes seems to be almost forgotten, at least within the framework of the historical narrative.[2] The transition is made between the two forms of the tradition by our being told briefly at the beginning of the Book of Exodus (Ex. 1.1–7) that the sons of Jacob who had come to Egypt had expanded naturally into a great multitude.

It is obvious that here the evolution of a nation is being described in an apparently casual but actually highly simplified way – a process which cannot historically have taken place so easily. But this kind of account becomes explicable when we bear in mind that the story of the patriarchs, which had up to then been considered as mere family history, had to be fused together with the accounts of events in Egypt, which patently presupposed and knew the nation as a completed entity. For the historian this observation is an extremely significant one. He is bound to conclude from the different types of account used for the story of the patriarchs and the Egypt complex that there were different conditions of transmission in each case, that they developed out of independent historical milieus, but that both were ultimately closely related to the later Israel.

This discrepancy in form between the traditions about the patriarchs and the Egypt traditions had far-reaching consequences for the content of the different complexes as well. If the two traditions are viewed in succession to one another, the sojourn in Egypt by the sons of Jacob (i.e. the later Israel) appears as the result of the acute difficulties experienced by Jacob's family. Famine made his sons journey into Egypt; the fact that they finally came to remain there, together with their father Jacob, was connected with the fortunes of Joseph. But how does this course of events tie up with the promise of land and descendants made to the patriarchs? Had this not already been fulfilled when the patriarchs Abraham, Isaac and Jacob established themselves in central and southern Palestine, and lived there for so many years? And must they not have had the justifiable hope that what they had been told – that is to say the constitution of the future nation – was directly taking place there? But now Jacob leaves the land of promise with his family and moves into distant parts, with the prospect of an uncertain future. Apart from this, however, Moses is again promised the very same land which the patriarchs possessed as the country where the elements of the nation which are menaced in Egypt are to find rest. It is true that this is exactly the Pentateuch's view, but it is still a highly open and important question whether the promise to the patriarchs was really, from the very beginning, thought of as being fulfilled circuitously, by way of Egypt and via a second promise to Moses. It is significant that the wording of the two promises differs as well. The patriarchs are quite generally promised land and descendants; and through them all generations on earth are ultimately to be blessed. Moses, on the other hand, is assured that he will lead the people out of Egypt into a country 'flowing with milk and honey', a phrase which never fell to the share of the patriarchs before Moses. One can therefore justly talk about two types of promise,[3] which are used in strict separation from one another and must consequently also be assigned to independent blocks of tradition. The double promise of land and also, analogously, the double occupation – first by the patriarchs, later under the leadership of Moses – therefore rests on the hardly disputable secondary combination of two complexes of tradition, which can only be explained if we look for a background of different historical contexts as well.

Though this separation of the traditions is undoubtedly correct, and demands its own interpretation, historical research must not come to a standstill once the critical analysis of the tradition has arrived at such a result. We still have to explain how these apparently heterogeneous strands of tradition ultimately came to be combined. This also leads us to formulate the historical question in quite a new way: is, namely, the co-ordination of the Genesis and Exodus traditions and their interpretation as a single thread of salvation history (which is the ultimate concern of the pragmatic presentation in the Pentateuch) legitimate, not only from a theological point of view but also historically?

This already presents us, through observation of the texts themselves, with a number of criteria for the historical understanding of Israel's presence in Egypt. For it has to be explained how the patriarchs and their families are connected with the elements which had settled permanently in Egypt. We must expect that the process of Israel's evolution, which in the Pentateuch is conceived and presented in linear fashion, under the aspect of salvation history, was in reality more complex; and that the placing of the traditions about the patriarchs before the traditions about Egypt must be judged as being merely an attempt to co-ordinate what were originally independent developments. We must, in short, reckon with the possibility that a quite independent meaning must be assigned to the patriarchal complex, and that this is to be put on an equal level with the traditions about the period in Egypt; the patriarchs of Genesis were not merely a 'trailer' to the work of Moses – they had a complete history of their own. But if it is the case that Israel, to put it broadly, grew up out of two definite areas of tradition and life – the sphere of the patriarchs and the sphere probably dominated by Moses – then the historian will be bound to look for pre-conditions (which will first emerge independently of the biblical writings, from the history of the ancient East in the second half of the second millennium before Christ), in order to see ultimately whether and how the fate of early Israel can be fitted into these events; and whether and how the complexity of the biblical evidence can be explained. The meaning and importance of Israel's stay in Egypt will then emerge more clearly, and we shall see better how the details which contradict one another in the biblical account are to be adjusted – for example, the double tradition of the promise.

II

THE TIMES AND THEIR EVENTS

'he second half of the second millennium BC is regarded here as
eing the framework for the Genesis and Exodus traditions,
pparently as a matter of course. Scholars are virtually unanimous
1 the opinion that the period of the Egyptian king Ramesses II
hirteenth century BC) is the period which comes into question
or Israel's stay in Egypt, particularly for the time immediately
receding the exodus. They are not so unanimous about fitting the
atriarchs into the pattern of the migrations which took place in
1e second millennium BC. Until very recently, views were main-
ained which were based on the assumption that Abraham might
lready have lived in the first centuries of this millennium.[1] Here
1e decision can in any case only be made with a relative degree of
ertainty. But none the less, a whole series of observations makes
  possible to limit the span of time covered by the patriarchal
adition to a greater extent than many would hold to be correct.
'nfortunately no non-biblical source tells us anything about any
f the patriarchs. Even Moses is not mentioned anywhere outside
1e Old Testament.[2] Consequently we are in every case dependent
n indirect conclusions. The prerequisite for such conclusions is a
etailed knowledge of the historical circumstances and context.
1 the second millennium BC these are particularly complicated and
ultifarious; but they can be defined and their peculiar character
rasped through steady research and the increasing opening up of
nportant source material from the whole area of the ancient East.
  We have to start from the basic fact that in the second millennium
1e Near East was shaken and troubled by numerous infusions of
opulation, which varied in origin and consequence. They were
oncentrated mainly on the cultivated lands bordering the Arabian

peninsula on the north, an area which is familiarly summed up as
the 'Fertile Crescent'. This includes the Mesopotamian region in
its full extent, the 'land of the two rivers', the Tigris and the
Euphrates, and it also covers the Syrian area that adjoins the
western part of Mesopotamia on the south. This Syrian region is
usually divided into a northern section, Syria proper, and a
southern part, Palestine. Egypt, being an already established great
power at this time, played an independent role, but did not of
course remain untouched by developments among its neighbours.
The infusions of population into the countries of the Fertile
Crescent came both from the south, from the desert and steppe
regions of the Arabian peninsula, and from the north, from the
ranges of those mountainous countries which border Mesopotamia towards the north, including the area of Asia Minor. In the
countries we have mentioned, these movements led in part to the
formation of important concentrations of power, but they never
remained undisputed. New conquerors prevailed and for a time
determined developments over a larger or smaller territory.

As early as the first decades of the second millennium BC something took place on the Egyptian east delta frontier which can be
called prototypical for an important part of Egyptian history in
the centuries that followed. The first ruler of the twelfth Egyptian
dynasty, Amenemhet I (1991–1962 BC), built the 'Prince's Wall',[3]
an extensive series of fortifications surmounted by numerous
watchtowers, against apparently large contingents of intruding
Bedouins who, coming from the Sinai peninsula in to the eastern
delta, found free access to the cultivated lands of Egypt. That this
wall was admittedly not a completely impenetrable 'iron curtain' we
learn from a contemporary document, the Tale of Sinuhe;[4] this
prominent Egyptian government official left Egypt in a hurry after
receiving news of the sudden death of Amenemhet, and reached
the Sinai desert, and ultimately the area of Syria-Palestine, by way
of the eastern delta. Sinuhe was the only one to break out of
Egypt through the Prince's Wall. He himself describes in dramatic
terms how careful he had to be and the dangers to which he was
exposed:[5]

I gave (free) road to my feet going northward, and I came up to the
Wall-of-the-Ruler, made to oppose the Asiatics and to crush the Sand-
Crossers. I took a crouching position in a bush, for fear lest the watch-
men upon the wall where their day's (duty) was might see me. I set out

at evening time, and when day broke I reached Peten. I halted at the Island of Kem-wer [the area of the Bitter Lakes]. An attack of thirst overtook me. I was parched, and my throat was dusty. I said: 'This is the taste of death!' (But then) I lifted up my heart and collected myself, for I had heard the sound of the lowing of cattle, and I spied Asiatics. The sheikh among them, who had been in Egypt, recognized me. Then he gave me water while he boiled milk for me. I went with him to his tribe. What they did (for me) was good.

This friendly reception by the Bedouins (whose worldly-wise sheikh immediately recognized the famous Sinuhe) may not be without a conscious literary and factual bias,[6] but the accompanying details are characteristic of the situation of the time. Large-scale movements of Bedouins are taking place beyond the frontier along the eastern delta. Amenemhet I's drastic defence measures already form a climax in the struggle against these intruding foreign elements. A hundred years earlier King Achthoes III had already found some hard things to say about the Bedouin nuisance in the east (in a wisdom teaching addressed to his son Merikare), and he exhorted his heir to take vigorous measures. It is interesting that in this historical section of the *Instruction for King Merikare*,[7] as it is called, the royal exhortation is linked with a revealing account of the characteristics and living conditions of the advancing desert-dwellers:[8]

Lo, the wretched Asiatic – it goes ill with the place where he is, afflicted with water, difficult from many trees, the ways thereof painful because of the mountains. He does not dwell in a single place, (but) his legs *are made to go astray*. He has been fighting (ever) since the time of Horus,[9] (but) he does not conquer, not yet can he be conquered. He does not announce a day in fighting, like *a thief* who . . . for a gang.

Then the king turns firmly to his son.

But as I live! I am while I am![10] The bowmen, however, are a locked wall, opened . . . I made the Northland smite them, I captured their inhabitants, and I took their cattle, to the disgust of the Asiatics against Egypt. Do not trouble thyself about him: he is (only) an Asiatic, *one despised* on his (own) coast. He may rob a single *person*, (but) he does not lead against a town of many citizens.

Then there is apparently talk about particular defence measures.

Dig a dyke against [half] of it as far as the Bitter Lakes. Behold, it is the (very) navel-cord of foreigners. Its walls are warlike, and its soldiers are many.

The text (which is not consistently well preserved) describes the constant and incalculable danger of the Bedouins from the eastern desert, and it also seems already aware of something like measures of defence (ramparts, dikes, ditches, etc.), which we should probably not be far wrong in supposing were forerunners of the 'walls of the ruler' which Amenemhet I built, thereby at last successfully banishing the most severe threats. It is not without triumph that another text points out as something redounding to Amenemhet's credit[11] that the king had seen to it that the Bedouins had once again to beg for water in the prescribed manner. This was the way things ought to be; this, from the perspective of the sated and superior inhabitant of a cultivated land, was thought of as being the ideal state of affairs; these tribes who, with their herds, sought for favourable grazing places and water on the fringes of the cultivated lands, should not take such things for themselves, but should be forced to beg for them!

How long Amenemhet's Prince's Wall survived and how effective it remained we do not know. It is certain that the thrusts from the eastern delta did not cease. It must indeed be assumed that there was a successive infiltration of elements of the population from the adjoining parts of Asia, which continually increased during the Egyptian Middle Kingdom, in the twentieth and nineteenth centuries BC and later. There is a good deal of evidence for this which shows that men and women from the region of Syria and Palestine came to Egypt and even penetrated into certain trades and professions, actually achieving leading positions.[12] This at first peaceful infiltration was replaced, however, by a stronger, aggressive thrust which was fateful for Egypt and brought about the end of the Middle Kingdom. A ruling caste which had penetrated the eastern delta succeeded in forming a government of its own there and in seizing control of Egypt for itself for several dynasties. These were the people known as the Hyksos.

The origin, nature and manner of their penetration still presents scholars with a particularly difficult problem. It has been established that the Greek term for this ruling caste, Hyksos (which goes back to Manetho's account of the history of Egypt,[13] where it was translated by 'shepherd kings'), is identical with the Egyptian expression *ḥqꜣ.w ḫꜣś.wt*, 'ruler of foreign lands', which was later simplified into the Greek form 'Hyksos'. The term is already used during the Middle Kingdom for tribal chiefs from around Syria. For that reason there is extensive agreement among scholars that the Hyksos made their thrust at Egypt from the north and that Palestine and Syria must basically have been their recruiting and assembly ground. But opinions are divided as to how firm the internal unity of these elements was in the period before their invasion of Egypt – whether they possessed an independent kingdom of their own,[14] whether their action was connected with the movements of the Hurrians,[15] or whether we have to do with what was originally a ruling caste in the region of southern Syria.[16] It is certainly wise to conceive the concentration of these forces as taking place in a restricted area, rather than in the vast dimension of an extensive territorial, ethnic and political unity. The possibility cannot be excluded that the final massing of their powers before the invasion of Egypt was due to the purposeful intention of certain small groups, who were also in a position for successful military action.[17] The Hyksos problem cannot be solved here, but it plays a part in the whole theme with which we are concerned, because it is obviously tempting to relate this movement directly, or even more remotely, to the movements of the Old Testament patriarchs.

This latter possibility, however, seems to have little probability in its favour, if only because the Hyksos were finally expelled by the rulers of Upper Egypt,[18] and the remembrance of them died out almost completely in the period that immediately followed. After the Hyksos period Egypt entered upon one of its great eras of expansion, which took its armies not only into the Nubian south but above all also into the region of Palestine and Syria. True, in the Egyptian New Kingdom which now dawned, the eastern delta still continued more or less intensively to be the goal and 'catchment' area for Bedouin elements; but it was above all the gateway from which the Egyptian troops and their generals and kings sallied forth to expand (with varying success) the lordship of Egypt almost as far as Syria and nearly to the Mesopotamian border. This development reached its first peak in the eighteenth dynasty, through the campaigns of Kings Thutmosis I and Thutmosis III (fifteen century BC). This brings us to the middle of the second millennium. Before considering the course of Egyptian history any further, however, we ought to cast a brief glance at the no less eventful, though in many respects more obscure, history of the Mesopotamian region in the first centuries of the second millennium before Christ.

In fact, movements parallel to the infiltration process on the Egyptian north-east frontier also took place on a broad front from the Syrian and Arabian desert area, though their complexity is so great, and the source material connected with them is so diffused, that the unity and homogeneity of the incidents may with reason be doubted. Attempts have been made to establish the relative coherence of this great Semitic movement (as it must be called), particularly by drawing on linguistic evidence. Here it is possible to point out common features of vocabulary and structure which are to be found in the scattered cuneiform material belonging to this period, and which were deposited in various records and documents when these new racial elements came into contact with the already established population. This great Semitic movement, which goes back to the beginning of the millennium, has in the course of time been given various names by oriental scholars who, taking linguistic features as their starting point, also wanted to claim an ethnic movement, terminologically and in actual fact. In earlier research especially, these ethnic elements were summed up as 'Amorites';[19] soon after, because of common linguistic features, they were defined as 'East Canaanites'[20] or 'West Semites';[21] and finally, with the support of new textual finds from Mari on the middle Euphrates, they were interpreted as 'Proto-Aramaeans'.[22] All these names are ultimately only expedients, each of which perhaps does little more than match the character of a particular section of this movement, and is not quite independent of the scholarly position out of which it developed. What is indisputable is a series of historical events whose origin we are simply bound to see as being constant new encroachments on particular Mesopotamian territories.

In the context of these events (although we cannot develop them in detail here), we must first review the rise of what is known as the first dynasty of Babylon (*c.* 1830–1530 BC). The sixth king of this dynasty was the famous Hammurabi (1728–1686), who is generally less well known today for his military successes than for his collection of laws.[23] Almost at the same time, the state of Asshur, the city state on the middle Tigris,[24] experienced its first great zenith, which was yet to convulse the eastern world so terribly; and here a counterpart at least equal to Hammurabi arose in Shamshi-adad I. But he was not to remain Hammurabi's only opponent. At the same time strong warlike elements from the Elamite mountains threatened Babylon from the east. Hammurabi was able to defeat their king, Rim-sin of Larsa, while the death of the Assyrian king put an end to the dangers from the north-west. The kingdom of Mari, through whose conquest the Assyrians had gained an important increase in power, finally also succumbed to Babylon's superior strength.

Almost at the same time as the downfall of the Hyksos in Egypt, Hammurabi's splendid dynasty also approached its end. A new era for Mesopotamia approached. Peoples from the mountain countries of the north pushed forward towards Mesopotamia. A raid made by Hittites under their king Mursilis I – that is to say from remote Asia Minor – robbed the Babylonians of their independence. About the middle of the millennium the rise of the so-called 'mountain peoples', the Kassites, Hurrians and Hittites, determined the face of Babylonian and Assyrian history. They achieved independent kingdoms; the Hurrians, for example, in close association with Indo-Aryan elements, founded the state of Mitanni[25] in the second half of the sixteenth century and reached out far not only into the Mesopotamian area but also into northern Syria.

Whereas the Mesopotamian region with its history thus sank into a darkness of succeeding foreign dominations round about the middle of the millennium, Egypt reached out beyond its frontiers in a hitherto unprecedented way, successfully achieving its greatest extension of power, from southern Nubia to far in the north – at its peak as far as the banks of the Euphrates. The Hyksos were driven out, and under the eighteenth dynasty and its rulers, who then came to power (rulers among whom the names Amenophis and Thutmosis predominate),[26] the Egyptians penetrated deep into the area of Palestine and Syria. The intensity of these ventures certainly varied; but none the less Egyptian power in Syria and Palestine was able to survive down to the last centuries of the millennium. Even today the lists of conquered cities on the walls of Egyptian temples witness to the military renown of the Pharaohs. Of particular interest among these lists are the ones which present us with series of places in Palestine and Syria, thus giving us a lively impression of the topographical situation of pre-Israelite Palestine.[27]

The Egyptians were unable to keep a permanent hold on what they had won. As time went by, they were increasingly bound to come up against the limits of their potential; as things were, these limits were set by the mountain peoples, who had meanwhile grown strong, and especially by the Hittites, who pushed forward as far as Syria, thereby directly infringing the Egyptian sphere of interest. But the internal development of Egypt did not remain free of crises either – and these were also bound to have an effect on external affairs. In the fourteenth century BC came the reign of the most remarkable of Egyptian rulers, who was to set his stamp on the attitude to life of a whole era, short-lived though that era was. This was the ruler who is known as the 'heretic' king, Amenophis IV, who chose to worship the solar disc, in the framework of an independent theological system,[28] rather than to follow the cult of the old familiar gods. Amenophis created his own capital, which was rediscovered near what is today *tell el-'amarna*,[29] and from that time called himself Akhenaten.[30] One should avoid acclaiming the undoubtedly individualist career of this king as the dawn of a kind of solar monotheism. For that, the 'faith of Amarna' remained ultimately still too imprisoned in Egyptian presuppositions, and it remains questionable whether we should concede to Akhenaten an act springing out of an unusual depth of perception, or whether we should not rather see the Amarna attitude to life as the far-off wildfire of a decline, the token of a late flowering inclined to the eccentric.[31]

If Amenophis IV's successor wrenched the helm round in another direction and forcibly extinguished all remembrance of the king, it was doubtless out of the feeling that here was the brink of a catastrophe. Egypt's activity in the field of foreign policy was flagging;[32] the country was even in danger of losing its independent role as leader. It is a sign of the times that the widow of Akhenaten's successor, the Tutankhamun whose tomb was later to become so famous,[33] sent two letters to the king of the Hittites, asking him to send her a prince whom she might wed. The Hittite prince set off, but never arrived. The military government which was at the helm in Egypt knew how to prevent it. For in fact a Hittite prince as husband of the king of Egypt's widow would have been in a position to unite the mightiest kingdoms of the time under a single hand and would thereby have been able to bring about political unity in the ancient East for the first time. Meanwhile the altercation with the Hittites was carried on in a different way. Akhenaten was among the last rulers of the eighteenth dynasty. The nineteenth dynasty made itself militarily strong once more and pursued an active policy, in Palestine and Syria as well. It was in this context that at the very beginning of the dynasty (possibly already under Sethos I, *c.* 1305–1290 BC, but certainly in the reign of his son Ramesses II, *c.* 1290–1223 BC)[34] the plan was pursued and largely realized of moving the capital of the empire away from the traditional metropolises, Thebes in the south and Memphis in the north, into the eastern delta, i.e., immediately at the gateway that led out to Palestine and Syria.[35] The consolidation of this new capital, which was given the name Ramesses, lasted at least as long as the period of the twentieth dynasty. Since the name also occurs in Ex. 1.11 as one of the few definite indications of place, this is an important clue, which is of extraordinary, if not uniquely decisive, importance for the localization and dating of the Israelites' stay in Egypt. We shall come back to this later.[36] At the moment the only essential point is to see the function of this delta residence of the Ramessids in the wider framework of the political and military intentions of the rulers of the nineteenth dynasty. They were in the course of setting up a centre for their power precisely between the motherland and its foreign possessions, which were threatened to an increasing degree, especially at first by the Hittites.

The period of Ramesses II itself brought some solution to the conflict with the Hittites. At Kadesh on the Orontes, that is to say in central Syria, the great powers fought a decisive battle, about which we have detailed information. The Egyptian tradition as it has been passed down to us even allows the tactical movements of the Hittites and Egyptians to be reconstructed.[37] It praises the valour of the king and his personal efforts, and gives the impression of a brilliant Egyptian victory. In fact, however, it was a trial of strength which demonstrated the power of both sides and did not allow a clear victor to be discerned. Egyptians and Hittites demarcated their spheres of influence more clearly than before; the border between the two lay in central Syria, as it had done earlier, possibly on the coast on the level of the *nahr-el kelb*.[38] The actual balance of power was ultimately sealed by what was for the ancient world a unique document – a proper peace treaty between Ramesses II and the Hittite king Ḫattušil III.[39]

But the balance of power arrived at by this means was not to endure for long. In an astonishingly short time this whole power structure was completely destroyed by new movements which broke in from outside and fundamentally changed the political field of force. These movements were the advance from the west of what are called the Sea Peoples and, from the east, a new massing of elements seeking land. Coming from the Syrian and Arabian desert, the latter reached the Fertile Crescent on a broad front and engaged in what were, according to circumstances, more or less severe struggles with the established rulers, This great new movement from the region of the Syrian and Arabian desert is generally summed up under the name 'Aramaeans'; their original precursors may count as being the desert-comers to whom Mari texts already witness in the eighteenth century BC. [40] This means that the area of Syria and Palestine was reached in rapid succession by two movements, which contributed to a complete revolution in the previous balance of power there and gradually completely eliminated the already diminishing influence of those great powers which had been in the ascendancy up to that period.

The kingdom of the Hittites, together with its tributary states in northern Syria, as well as the Canaanites of Palestine (and earlier, perhaps, the representatives of the Cretan-Mycenaean civilization also), fell victims to an onslaught of peoples – an onslaught which was directed (though not exclusively) over the eastern Mediterranean towards Asia Minor, Syria and Palestine, and not least Egypt, where in its turn it unleashed attacks on Egypt by Libyan tribes. The points of departure of these intruders cannot be determined with certainty and the details of their advance also elude us; but its usual description, the migration of the Sea Peoples, probably describes accurately enough the main direction, at least, of their coming, from the perspective of those who were affected. Ramesses III did in fact have to meet them in a sea battle. The penetration of the Philistines into the coastal plains of Palestine (where Egyptian power had meanwhile succumbed completely) is ultimately viewed as part of this migration of the Sea Peoples. This went a good way towards marking out the power relationships in the Canaanite area with which the Israelites were to have to do right down to the period of the kings. The Philistines made good their position in the coastal areas, while they at first neglected the mountainous hinterland.

But these mountains west and east of the Jordan, far less densely populated by the Canaanites, were still open to the grasp of the immigrants coming from the east. This was the country which the wave of Aramaean migration now neared; and the facts prompt an essential question; what elements of this great group of Aramaean peoples coming from the east now reached the terrain east and west of the Jordan and looked to find a home there? The historically correct answer to this question is that it was the tribes 'of Israel' which now appeared on the stage of world history. But how did this come about, and what did the groups look like in detail? Was this a self-contained formation? Was it a single, clearly demarcated event of limited duration? These are the problems of 'Israel's' early history, which have been the subject of discussion down to the present day and which have been differingly interpreted at different times. They appear in a differing light not least because the Old Testament itself (which alone is in a position to throw light on these events) does not make an unequivocal answer possible in all respects. Self-contained movements, such as those in the Book of Joshua, stand side by side with individual actions; the Book of Joshua also indicates the latter in places, but they are passed down to us primarily in the Book of Judges. Here we have, for example, the way in which individual tribes react and gather together in order to meet the attacks of other tribal units and peoples.

But what is the relation between these relatively compact actions in the Books of Joshua and Judges on the one hand and the patriarchs with their families on the other? For the stories about the occupation of the promised land in the historical books from Joshua onwards never refer back to the patriarchs at all. It is true that Deuteronomy testifies clearly to the Aramaean descent of the patriarchs (Deut. 26.5), but what about the other tribes? Can they be tacitly absorbed into the same genealogical line of descent? Must they not in fact be included in this line of descent if we take seriously what the genealogical lists and tables of affinities in Genesis suggest – that the Israelite tribes were directly related to one another, as the sons of Jacob? But the question remains whether this relationship was a fore-given and self-evident one from the very beginning, or whether the genealogical tables themselves did not have the purpose of creating and substantiating a relationship which only grew out of a later stage of history, and which did not exist from the outset. In other words: do the genealogical tables of the patriarchs and their families reflect an originally genuine connection, or are they an attempt to give a subsequent reason, and hence legitimation, for the cohesion of a twelve-tribe system which grew up in Palestine? These are certainly very serious questions, to which we must at this point add a supplementary one: how, in the face of these facts, are we to assess the people who lived in Egypt and took their departure from there, with the promised land as their goal?

The complexity of the questions, which in its turn rests on the complexity of the biblical traditions, should by no means discourage us at the outset. For the very complexity of the Old Testament's presentation of history fits in very well at this point with the evidently highly complex reshuffling of power relationships in Syria and Palestine towards the end of the second millennium BC. The one important thing is to survey and classify the trend of tradition and historical probability in such a way that it is possible to reconstruct from it a historical development and course of events that has a high degree of plausibility in its favour, and that can also be fitted as smoothly as possible into the various sources. This inevitably means that we have to set ourselves the task of treating the story of the Israelite tribes in Egypt as adequately as possible against the background of the historical events of the second millennium BC, as we have indicated them above (especially the power revolution that took place after the invasion of the Sea Peoples), and of interpreting the sources at our disposal with constant reference to the great developments of the period.

III

ISRAEL IN EGYPT IN THE FRAMEWORK OF WORLD HISTORY

A detailed investigation, carried out against the background of developments as a whole in the second millennium BC, confirms in a surprising way what the biblical evidence suggests. The particular forms of transmission (the patriarch traditions as family history on the one hand; the tradition about Egypt, as the history of a whole people on the other) also cover two different geographical areas, each with its particular trend of development. The roving patriarchs with their herds, who gradually find a footing in cultivated lands, whose wanderings take place between Mesopotamia and Syria–Palestine, fit excellently, structurally speaking, in their whole semi-nomadic character[1] into the Mesopotamian milieu. More precisely, they fit in with those elements of the population which, coming from the Syrian and Arabian desert, gradually gained ground wherever they came upon less thickly settled lands in the cultivated country. This may apply, roughly speaking, to the country in north-west Mesopotamia, the area round Haran where, according to the evidence of Gen. 11.28ff., Abraham's kindred settled before they reached Palestine, but where it can also be shown that strong Aramaean contingents attained power.[2] It seems entirely possible, however, that – especially in the border areas of north-west Mesopotamia and in North Syria – individual families were forced out into southern Syria at the time when the Aramaean states began to take shape, from about the thirteenth century BC onwards. The Aramaean 'ready to perish' of Deut. 6.5 (AV), who according to this passage was Israel's ancestor,[3] could certainly have belonged to the Aramaean wandering tribes, but could have been unable, contrary to his expectations, to take the first step towards settlement, either in the Mesopotamian or in the Syrian border region. It was only in the Palestinian area that he found certain preconditions for taking possession of land in the Philistine hinterland.

What Genesis 13 describes is in fact a typical situation. Everyone had to look for the best that the land had to offer. Lot believed that he had found it in the fruitful Jordan valley, in the oasis of Jericho, but he later came into conflict with the native inhabitants of Sodom, where there must have been a fairly strong Canaanite enclave.[4] Abraham was able to come to terms better with the people of Hebron and its surroundings. Here stages in the occupation of a country are put on record in the form of a family history – stages which can be easily explained in the wake of the revolution in population and power relationships which took place in the Canaanite hinterland at about the same time as the Sea Peoples' thrust from the west, untouched though the area was at first by the invasion.

What can clearly be said in this way about the patriarchs and their families, structurally and also chronologically, is by analogy predictable and plausible for the stay in Egypt of certain Semitic groups. For there is no doubt that these groups penetrated no deeper into Egypt than the eastern delta. 'Israel's' stay in Egypt, even on the basis of the biblical evidence, can only be explained within the complex of tradition about Semitic infiltrations from the Sinai desert, which could basically be observed as early as the beginning of the millennium. That these groups did not now apparently penetrate beyond the eastern delta further towards Egypt, but already fell into the 'house of bondage' there (Ex. 20.2), being requisitioned for building operations (Ex. 1), can also be explained quite plausibly from the time of the nineteenth Egyptian dynasty. For the Pharaohs of the time, these Semitic groups came at just the right moment to help in the building of the new capital which they were setting up at the gateway to Palestine. That Ex. 1.11 even goes so far as to say that the Israelites were set to build 'store-cities' also fits into the overall picture. For these store-cities must simply have been the domestic buildings and warehouses for the maintenance of the Pharaoh's new court, in the area surrounding the city of Ramesses. The two places named in Ex. 1.11, Pithom and Raamses, document this as clearly as one could wish. We shall consider this in detail later. At the moment we mention it only because it is important to show that the time spent in Egypt by what were later Israelite elements also appears in a connection which is convincing in the framework of world history and is at the same time closely related, chronologically and factually, to the movements of the patriarchs within the Aramaean context.

But before we attempt to define more closely the relationship of the two different movements, the patriarchs on the one hand and the Semites in Egypt on the other, we must cast a brief glance, at least, at other attempts at a solution, which are still accepted down to the present day by scholars of repute and which are apparently supported by convincing arguments, even if their provisional character is sometimes admitted. The main difference between these answers and the view expounded here lies in the differing conception of the chronological and geographical extent of the events. Some scholars have believed that they were bound to connect the patriarchs with movements as great and as far back as possible. Albright, for example (though his view has already met with strong opposition), has suggested that Abraham ought to be placed in the broad context of the caravan merchants who already had their fixed routes between Mesopotamia and Egypt in the nineteenth century BC.[5] According to this interpretation, therefore, the journeys of the patriarchs between Mesopotamia and the Nile ought really to be seen against the background of these world-wide trade links. So Albright maintains, although none of the patriarchs known to us appears to be the trading member of a caravan.[6] This bold hypothesis is undoubtedly untenable; and the connection between the patriarchs and the Hyksos movement (which is continually asserted) cannot be supported either.[7] It is, of course, tempting to link up Abraham's repeatedly attested journey, and ultimately Jacob's journey into Egypt as well,[8] with this great movement from Syria and Palestine to the Nile. But on the other hand it is impossible to find a single warlike feature about the patriarchs; we miss every form of the urge towards expansion, in the sense of a culturally potent ruling class, which was capable of setting up a supremacy in Egypt. Ultimately this assertion raises more questions than it solves: the Hyksos were driven out – they lost influence almost at a stroke; and in the following centuries there poured out through the eastern delta the Egyptian armies which conquered Palestine and Syria. What role was played here by the 'Israelites' who came with the Hyksos? Where and how did they survive, before determining to leave Egypt once more under the Ramessids? Who preserved their traditions about their first occupation of land at Hebron and Bethel, and in what way? Who could have had any interest in preserving these traditions for several centuries, and for what purpose? For between the Hyksos and the Ramessids there gapes too vast a gulf of time – one which can hardly be convincingly bridged, especially if one wants to assume a certain continuity in the transmission of tradition which must have existed between the patriarchs and the later groups which had emigrated from Egypt.

Under the presuppositions of this large-scale thinking, there has been no lack of attempts to link up certain strange highlights of the Egyptian New Kingdom with the Israelites. The Amarna period offers a point of attack which is eagerly seized on. Moses himself has been transferred to the milieu of Akhenaten, not only because so extravagant a spirit would seem to be capable of suffering even a Moses, but because Moses himself might have taken ideas from him. The question has been seriously discussed whether the faith of Amarna, with its supposedly monotheistic tendency, helped to mould Moses' picture of God, and whether Yahweh's uniqueness grew ultimately out of the religious premises of this peculiar Egyptian development.[9] Quite apart from the fact that Akhenaten's successors ruthlessly undertook the rooting out of all remembrance of the 'heretic' of Amarna, we know that Akhenaten's form of belief was by no means so unequivocally monotheistic, and was therefore hardly capable of triggering off the epoch-making consequences ascribed to it, least of all in a man like Moses, who was certainly no Egyptian.[10]

These and similar attempts to link up the patriarchs, Moses and the Israelites with the principal events and figures of world history must be rejected as being more or less speculative. Their main error is probably the assumption that the Genesis and Exodus traditions extended over too great a space of time; their search for particular ethnological movements within this extensive period corresponding roughly to the wanderings of the patriarchs is also wrong. In contrast, the view I shall be expounding here is that the narrow complex of Old Testament tradition is only comprehensible and credible in a narrower temporal and geographical continuity. This means that the patriarchs, too, must be moved up very close to the events in Egypt and that the sojourn in Egypt itself was not a matter of centuries but was perhaps only an episode in which a few groups of what was later Israel were involved. The advantage of this viewpoint is that individual historical events must be, and can be, more closely considered than the large-scale hypotheses (which settle for a date between the nineteenth and thirteenth centuries BC) find necessary. The 'small-scale' solution is possible – and is even imperative – because it is incomparably more just to the Old Testament material than the vision which ranges into perspectives which are extensive but burdened by difficulties in detail.

This brings us back to the more detailed investigation of the postulates of the sojourn in Egypt of Semitic groups during the Ramessid period. It has become clear that the question of this stay hangs together very substantially with the problem of how these Semitic groups came to be in Egypt at all. It is customary to talk about the 'exodus' from Egypt. This exodus stands out in the Old Testament as a momentous event, and was decisive for Israel. Yet it was only the result of a development about which the Old Testament unfortunately does not talk, or only hints – how, in fact, the 'entry' into Egypt took place at all. The question is, whether it is permissible to deny these 'Proto-Israelites'[11] any connection with the 'Proto-Aramaean' groups of the patriarchs from the outset; or whether on the Egyptian eastern frontier as well population elements did not turn up which stood in a fairly close relationship to the Aramaean groups. Failing this, are these Egyptian elements later supposed to have attached themselves of their own accord to Bedouin groups which then took them to Palestine?

The representatives of the 'large-scale' theory support it very largely by pointing to linguistic connections, in the formation of proper names among other things.[12] Here points in common appear regularly in the observation of linguistic strata connected with people coming from the Syrian and Arabian desert. They display the linguistic elements which could also lead to the assumption of more or less close ethnic groupings, such as the terms 'Western Semites' or 'Proto-Aramaeans' are supposed to indicate more closely.[13] The linguistic characteristics which have been observed among these groups also include points in common in the formation of proper names, which show that the names of the patriarchs fit structurally into these contexts. Abraham represents a type of this kind[14] and so do the names Yiṣḥaq (Isaac) and Yaʿakōb (Jacob),[15] which are characterized by their prefigured *yod*. These principles of name-formation could lead us to the conclusion that the patriarchs themselves must also be shifted into the period when they first occur. There is no occasion for such an over-hasty solution. The elements which form the names retained their currency down to Old Testament times,[16] not least because they owe their origin to the principles common to the formation of Semitic names as a whole, that is to say, are connected with the incursion at various times of peoples from the Arabian desert. Proto-Aramaeans, Aramaeans and Israelites, different though they may be individually, none the less share in the common ground of their origin. So linguistic indications are able to give only partial information about historical events.

It is therefore all the more noteworthy that these and similar principles in the formation of names and words are found not only in the environment of the patriarchs but also among the southern groups which play a part in connection with the Exodus tradition. We cannot go into this in detail here,[17] but it must at least be pointed out that in all probability the divine name Yahweh itself belongs within the compass of these short-name formations with prefixed *yod*.[18] Other proper names that must be viewed as being compounded with the name Yahweh (which, that is to say, contain components of the name Yahweh as theophorous elements) can be definitely attested in Israel only from the period of the judges.[19] Whether elements of the basic forms out of which the name of Yahweh is composed are to be found, not only in the latitudes of southern Palestine, but also in Aramaean and Akkadian sources deriving from regions further north, is a disputed question of its own.[20] The essential point is that even the names given in the sphere of the 'Egypt' tribes (apart from the name of Moses) do not transgress the common principles governing Semitic names, and that this fact also offers a foundation for assuming ethnic points in common with the Aramaean movement, even for the so-called 'Egyptian' tribes.

Unfortunately we know too little about the precise operations of Aramaean groups in the southern part of the Fertile Crescent in the second half of the second millennium. Whether it is permissible also to read into this context the movements of those Bedouin groups which crop up in the Egyptian sources of the period under the name *š3s.w* (Shasu), is a question which has not been adequately clarified up to now – one, perhaps, which is incapable of complete clarification. [21] None the less, it corresponds with the period and its conditions, if even Egyptian sources record an increased Bedouin activity in and near the Sinai peninsula; and it is, again, a tempting but still too uncertain hypothesis to connect up the *š3s.w Yhw3* (i.e., the 'Shasu of' or 'from Yahweh'), who are recorded several times in Egyptian lists, with early Yahweh worshippers among the Aramaean tribes. [22] It is unfortunately still insufficiently clear whether this name 'Yahweh' apparently attested in Egyptian can really have anything to do with the Yahweh of the Old Testament. But it will none the less be permissible to talk, however cautiously, about an interesting name-formation which could also have been constitutive for the genesis of the divine name Yahweh. That the Shasu Bedouins were, however, by no means confined to the desert regions round about the Sinai peninsula, but that these movements reached as far as the eastern delta, and even penetrated the delta itself, is evidenced by a document which is important in many respects. This document is a letter to his superior officer from a frontier official stationed on the border of the eastern delta. The letter, which dates from *c.* 1192 BC, gives direct information about the frontier movements which had been taking place. [23] It runs:

Another communication to my [lord], to [wit: We] have finished letting the Shasu tribes of Edom[24] pass the Fortress [of] Mer-ne-Ptah[25] Hotep-hir-Maat – life, prosperity, health! – which is (in) Tkw,[26] to the pools of Per-Atum [of] Mer-[ne]-Ptah Hotep-hir-Maat, which are (in) Tkw, to keep them alive and to keep their cattle alive, through the great *ka* of Pharaoh – life, prosperity, health! – the good sun of every land, in the year 8,[27] 5 [intercalary][28] days, [the Birth of] Seth.[29]

I have had them[30] bring in a copy of the *report* to the [place where] my lord is, *as well as* the other names of days when the Fortress of Mer-ne-Ptah Hotep-hir-Maat – life, prosperity, health! which is (in) Tkw, may be passed.

Even though this frontier official's report dates from a period which was probably a little later than the 'exodus' of the Moses group, it reflects clearly and very vividly the situation on the east delta frontier during the nineteenth dynasty. Shasu Bedouins from Edom, that is to say probably from the area south of the Dead Sea, or at least near there, [31] have crossed the Sinai peninsula and reached the eastern delta with their herds. They pass the Egyptian guards (which is to say that they pass them with government consent), are registered, with an exact notation of the date, and, with the consent

of the Pharaoh, are given access to a favourable grazing place for
their herds. What we have here, therefore, is an official limited
frontier traffic for the use of officially authorized grazing places.
We may remember the passage from the prophecy of Neferti, at
the beginning of the millennium, which considers it to be a normal
state of affairs for the eastern Bedouins to beg for water in the prescribed way.³² In the time of the Ramessids the Bedouin frontier
traffic took its ordered course. The final note in the frontier
official's letter reveals that a certain trust was placed in the desert
dwellers. As well as their own registration note, they are permitted
to take the reports of the preceding period, with notes on the
frontier traffic which has taken place, to the frontier officer on
duty, who is at a point further inland. There is nothing to prevent
us from conceiving the penetration into Egypt of subsequent
Israelite tribal groups as taking place in the same way. This is
further emphasized by another circumstance as well.

The places mentioned in the frontier official's report lead us to
exactly the same area which was also, according to the biblical
evidence, the place where the 'Israelites' were. The name Pithom is
mentioned in Ex. 1.11. According to modern scholars, this name
probably hides the designation for a temple of the god Atum, near
which the pools mentioned also lay. The temple of Atum was
probably the centre of the place Tjeku,³³ which must be localized
on the *tell el-mashūta* in the eastern delta, in the fertile region of
wādi eṭ-ṭumēlāt. One is inclined to look here for an actual centre of
the grazing places offered by the favourable nature of the fertile
country, to which arriving Bedouins were directed.³⁴ This would
also seem to be the countryside that is meant by the term 'the land
of Goshen', which is several times declared to have been the area
which Pharaoh allotted to Jacob and his sons.³⁵ In addition, however, we find the name 'the land of Ramesses' (Gen. 47.11), and
we are bound to ask how this name ties up with the city of
Ramesses already mentioned.

The simplest answer would seem to be that 'Ramesses' or – if
we take account of Hebrew spelling – 'Raʿamses' was the name
both for the capital in the narrower sense and for the whole
district surrounding it. In fact, scholars have come up against
numerous questions in connection with this capital city built in
the delta by the rulers of the nineteenth dynasty – questions which
cannot be fully discussed here.³⁶ They begin with the full names

of this capital, one of which runs, *Pr-R'mššw-mrj-Imn-'3-nḫtw*
'House of Ramesses, beloved of Amun, great in victorious might',
whereas Ex. 1.11 only mentions a brief Ra'amses. This abbreviated
form is less problematical than the paraphrase of the name in
Hebrew.[37] More important historically are the archaeological
problems which revolve round the city's precise site, opportunity
for hypothesis being offered by a number of finds at different
places. On the one hand scholars concentrated on the ruins of Tanis
(*ṣān el-ḥagar*), somewhat further north in the eastern delta, where
the remains of a temple were found, but no palace.[38] Conversely,
excavations in the *kantir* about 12 miles south of Tanis brought to
light a palace but no temple.[39] The theory has been suggested that
both cities ought to be seen as parts of an extensive capital, comparable with the extension of Amenophis IV's capital at *tell el-
'amārna*.[40] If the area of the city of Ramesses was extended in this
way it would also be understandable that 'store cities' (Ex. 1.11)
should be built on the outskirts, and certainly not only there, as
centres for the economic provisioning of the Pharaoh's royal
household; and that people were requisitioned for the building
wherever they could be found. That would be precisely the
historical site where the building activities of the later Israelites,
which are so dramatically described in Ex. 1, would have to be
conceived of as taking place. On the Egyptian side there was no
shrinking from employing infiltrating Bedouins as cheap labour
and in inflicting hard and unaccustomed tasks on them. It was
understandable enough that these Bedouins, who knew only the
free and independent life of the desert dweller,[41] should try to
escape from the Pharaoh's forced labour as soon as possible. That
this involved difficulties can well be imagined. Ultimately, no
doubt, it was only possible through actual flight.

Of course, these topographical and archaeological explorations
and reflections only have an indirect bearing on the actual event of
the stay in Egypt itself and the exodus of these Semitic groups from
there.[42] For no actual traces pointing directly to such a stay have
been found up to now; and indeed they can hardly be expected, in
view of the whole nature of Israel's stay, as we have indicated it
above. For nomadic groups, even on the fringes of cultivated
countries, are not accustomed to set up monuments for themselves, in the way of buildings and inscriptions. None the less,
however, the few local places which have come down to us in

connection with stay and exodus show what a short distance the
Bedouins who are in question can have penetrated into cultivated
country, and how little justification there is for believing them
capable of any considerable organized force. Thus far the very
place names may serve to confirm the basically temporary – indeed
positively fleeting – character of the time spent in Egypt by
elements of the later Israel.

If we make use of these historically verifiable details, it will be
possible for us to form a coherent picture of the events which
preceded the stay in Egypt and which finally, with a certain in-
evitability, brought it about. It has already been suggested above
that here we have to do with elements of the greater Aramaean
migratory movement. We may presuppose that this wave of
migration did not only reach the Mesopotamian and Syrian area,
but that its southern ramifications strove no less intensely towards
a cultivated country, in order to face a gradual process of permanent settlement there. The conditions existing in Mesopotamia and
Syria – and indeed even in Palestine – were not unfavourable to
this undertaking, because there small countries possessing an at
least limited capacity for absorption did present themselves. Things
must have looked different, however, for the southernmost off-
shoots of this wave of Aramaeans, who on the level of the Sinai
peninsula did not at first find any cultivated country but had to
cross the peninsula at the eastern edge of the delta. However, this
delta already belonged within the Pharaoh's sphere of influence;
and though it is true that he temporarily put grazing places at
their disposal, he would hardly have been prepared to help the
tribes to permanent settlement. Thus it was inevitable that these
Aramaean groups in the eastern delta were very soon forced to end
their stay once more – not without pressure from Pharaoh's
central government – and to withdraw into the desert. Ultimately
this stay in Egypt was a kind of attempt to acquire land which mis-
carried; it was the fate of a number of Aramaean groups to leave
cultivated land again, once they had attained it, and after a further
long stay in the desert to try once more to occupy land in Palestine,
an attempt which was finally successful.

This view of things makes a plausible explanation possible for
the to some extent heterogeneous elements in the Pentateuch
tradition, which can now be united into a convincing general
picture. Whereas the tradition of the patriarchs, which is localized

more to the north, reflects the forward thrust of Aramaean groups who were apparently able to press forward directly into the highlands of west Jordan, the Egypt traditions have to do with a southern offshoot of the Aramaean groups, which only arrived at the occupation of Palestine later than the patriarchs, in a roundabout way, via a period spent in Egypt. These facts actually find appropriate confirmation through the geography of the tribes in Palestine. For the so-called 'house of Joseph', which found a footing in the mountains of central Palestine, with its centre in Shechem, formed the latest group of immigrants. It also apparently brought with it the faith in Yahweh which in the course of time fused with the religion of the patriarchs.[43] We must therefore assume that the patriarchs did in fact carry out an occupation of their own and that the union with the group of Yahweh worshippers who came from the south only took place in Palestine.

This briefly outlined picture, complicated though its particular presuppositions may be, may perhaps seem to many who are familiar with the material to be a radical simplification of what were in reality more complex facts. More complex they may undoubtedly have been. But none the less, it is possible to show here the basic structural features which make possible a largely trustworthy general picture – a picture which does not originate merely in purely speculative combinations, but which can also be confirmed at a number of further points. For this the Old Testament traditions give a direct opportunity.

Within the traditions about the patriarchs in Genesis, there are at various points lists which purport to give information about the kindred and relationships of the patriarchs and their children. If we look at these traditions as a whole, they will be seen to form a clear, self-contained system, which is rounded off not only genealogically, but also geographically and ethnically. This system takes its point of departure from Abraham and his brothers Nahor and Haran. Abraham had three wives, whose sons or grandsons each formed groups of six or twelve children. Abraham's brother Nahor also had twelve sons, whereas only Moab and Ammon are mentioned as being the grandsons of Haran and children of Lot (Gen. 19.30–38). With striking completeness, these groups of Abraham's kindred are distributed along a line running north to south along the edge of the Arabian desert. It appears as follows: Nahor's twelve sons (Gen. 22.20–24) form one group in upper

Mesopotamia and northern Syria; the twelve sons of Jacob, who were to constitute the later Israel, occupy the central region of Palestine and its immediate surroundings (Gen. 29.31—30.24; 35.17); then come Lot's two sons, Moab and Ammon (Gen. 19.30–38), as well as the twelve sons of Esau (Gen. 36.10–14), who represent the Edomite league. The south is covered by the six sons whom Keturah bears Abraham (Gen. 25.1–4) and by the twelve sons of Ishmael, Hagar's son (Gen. 25.12–18). There is no doubt at all that here we have a thought-out system, the conscious conception of a cohesion of peoples, consistently depicted in genealogical terms. Genealogical thinking is put to the service of ethnographical definition. It will hardly be difficult to recognize the grouping that is defined in this historically plausible way. The members of the Aramaean movement here appear as Abraham's kindred, just as, in the wake of increasing consolidation, they probably also appeared to the Israelite consciousness as being an organized political structure. Although it is impossible to give the reasons in detail here, this genealogical survey can hardly be conceived as being earlier than the period when the Israelite states were formed – the time, that is to say, in which Israel was also ideally understood as being a unity of twelve tribes. [44]

But let us now leave on one side the conditions under which this systematic survey arose. We must still say something a little more detailed about the groupings into units numbering six or twelve members. [45] What is essential for our present context is that Abraham's southern relatives (in the shape of the sons of Keturah and Ishmael) reached into the very area which includes the borders of the Arabian desert as far as the Sinai peninsula, as well as the adjoining regions to the north and south. Thus Midian also perhaps belonged to the sons of Keturah. The Midianites, as camel nomads, had a further area into which they penetrated, which reached as far as Palestine; they play a part in the story of Joseph (Gen. 37.27f.), just as do the Ishmaelites, among whose kindred there are tribes and peoples which must be sought for still deeper in the area of the Arabian peninsula.

Together with Edom, Midian is of quite special interest for Israel's early history, because it is with the Midianites that Moses makes contact on his flight from Egypt, even marrying the daughter of a Midianite priest (Ex. 2.21). It is in immediate proximity to the Midianite area that Moses experiences the manifesta-

tion of the burning bush (Ex. 3.1ff.). This brings us to the extraordinarily important question of how it came about – or how we
can explain the fact – that Moses was able to lead the Israelites out
of Egypt at the command of the God Yahweh. According to the
account we have in the Book of Exodus, Moses experienced the
decisive revelation of Yahweh outside Egypt, in the desert, and
had then to convince his fellow-countrymen in Egypt of the
legitimacy of his call and the character of the God who called him
(Ex. 3).[46] Whether this course of events is entirely sound historically is difficult to prove, but cannot be entirely denied either. The
kernel of the problem is that Yahweh was apparently an already
existing power before the exodus from Egypt, and then increasingly
took on importance for the Egypt groups as well. We may take it
as certain that this God was already known to these groups before
their entry into Egypt, as a deity localized at a mountain in the
Midianite area. The Egyptian evidence about the Shasu *Yhw3*
(which reaches back into the period of Amenophis III, i.e., about
a hundred years before the exodus) could be a welcome support
for this 'early' existence of Yahweh, or at least a power bearing
the name, open to question though things may be in detail.[47]

All these considerations serve to support the basic conception
that, in the wake of the Aramaean movement, the Sinai peninsula
and its surroundings were also the scene of vigorous tribal activity
and that it was from these very groupings that the sections which
penetrated into Egypt were also recruited. It therefore does not
seem unusual that the latter regained a connection with these
groups once more, after they had left Egypt, a process in which
Moses' Midianite contacts can certainly have played a part. That
the Israelites wanted to leave Egypt in order to sacrifice to their
God in the wilderness (Ex. 3.18 and frequently elsewhere) may
reflect a connection which must be taken seriously between the
Egypt groups and other groups and organizations living in the
desert, a connection which may easily have been not only religious
but also ethnic in character. This passage at least clearly reflects
what we have tried to show here within a wider context: that the
Egypt groups are not to be seen in isolation, but as a part of ethnic
formations which had their centres of gravity outside Egypt in the
vicinity of the Sinai peninsula.

Against the background of these reflections, we must touch
briefly on two critical questions, which are unfailingly raised in

connection with the period spent in Egypt by Semitic groups: the role of Joseph in Egypt; and the designation of the Israelites in Egypt as 'Hebrews'.

The Joseph story in Genesis, with all its detail, suggests to the reader a largely reliable Egyptian milieu, behind which wider historical relationships and events seem to lie. There has been no lack of attempts to look for situations (and the corresponding evidence in Egyptian texts) where a Semite rose to a prominent position in Egypt's state and economy, playing a particular part during a period of famine. The circumstance that from the time of the Middle Kingdom individual Semites really were able to occupy privileged positions in Egypt,[48] has lent support to suppositions that Joseph too was an example of a *parvenu* of this kind. A text belonging to the period of Ramesses III – that is to say, a time very close to the Exodus – even names a 'Syrian' who in years of dearth had subjected the country to taxation[49] and who seems to be the positive prototype of Joseph.

These details may indeed have great fundamental importance, and it cannot be denied that such circumstances may also have influenced the shaping of the character of Joseph; but there is no immediate and direct evidence in the Egyptian texts which would confirm that the Joseph of the Bible was a historical phenomenon. Even the searching investigation of the Joseph story which was designed to support its historicity from the Egyptological aspect and which found as much as possible in it to be authentic, was not able to alter anything here.[50] It is of course remarkable that the Egyptian details which occur in the story fit into the period of the Egyptian New Kingdom, though not at all into the Hyksos period; and thus an early date for the Joseph story can also be excluded. On the other hand, the complex of the Joseph stories must be explained differently, out of Old Testament conditions, not Egyptian ones. Joseph must be judged first of all as the son of Jacob, whose two sons were Ephraim and Manasseh – who, incidentally, were born in Egypt according to the Genesis account (Gen. 41.50–52; 46.20) and who were especially blessed by Jacob (Gen. 48.1ff.). But Ephraim and Manasseh were the two chief tribes which, summed up under the name of 'the house of Joseph', found a footing as one of the last Israelite groups in the central mountains of west Jordan, with the town of Shechem as centre. From these tribes, too, essential stimuli for the spread of the

Yahweh religion proceeded. To put it cautiously, they were the core – or at least one of the most effective parts historically[51] – of the groups of tribes which came from the south. Joseph, who together with Benjamin was Rachel's son, counted as the father of the tribe. Both Joseph and Benjamin were born in exceptional circumstances.[52] There can be no doubt about the special position of these tribes, though the reasons cannot be given in detail here.[53] Joseph is a special case, in that the figure of an important tribal father of Israel is individually developed as a personality of particular quality and made the centre of a dramatic narrative whole. Joseph's characteristics as tribal father are by no means entirely obliterated here. This becomes quite obvious on a closer reading of Genesis 37–50. But the detailed, novellistic narrative emerges equally clearly as an independent construction, and can hardly have received its final form before the beginning of the Israelite monarchy. There is indeed much to be said in favour of supposing that the somewhat enlightened and culturally vigorous period of David and Solomon contributed to the story's final form. It has been shown on the basis of individual features of the account that Joseph is described as an ideal figure in the sense of ancient Israelite wisdom, his good conduct standing the test even in different situations of extremity.[54]

Seen as a whole, the story of Joseph in Genesis unites elements of ancient tribal tradition, which know Joseph as tribal father, with a far later novellistic form of presentation, which employs correctly observed Egyptian details, but which is in places also permeated by what are obvious Semitisms.[55] The Joseph story is ultimately a kind of *Bildungsroman*, a novel of psychological development, belonging to the 'open-minded' period of the kings; it knew how to represent the ancient fathers of the tribe as being the object of miraculous divine leadings, but it offers little more in the way of specific Egyptian local colour than could reasonably have been known outside Egypt about Egyptian conditions. Thus it is the chief witness to an Israelite picture of Egypt of astonishing perception; but its human and religious sensitivity is drawn from the Israelite spirit alone.

The second problem we have to deal with here relates to the fact that the Israelites are termed Hebrews, a name which can by no means be simply equated with 'Israelites', though this is not uncommon in a conventional, superficial way of talking.[56] The

Hebrew word '*ibrī*, which is generally translated by 'Hebrew', is actually very little used in the original Old Testament text; its use is confined mainly to the Pentateuch, and within the Pentateuch to the Books of Genesis and Exodus; eight passages in I Samuel, where the word appears in connection with the Philistines,[57] are the only exception. For our present purpose it is particularly important that the Genesis and Exodus passages, with two exceptions,[58] refer only to the Israelites in Egypt, that is to say they are confined to the Joseph story and to the exodus tradition passed down to us in Ex. 1–10.[59] This is undoubtedly a remarkable fact which demands a particular explanation. Scholars have up to now been virtually unanimous in the view that the Old Testament '*ibrī* must be identical with the word *ḫapiru* or *ḫabiru*, and with the Egyptian '*pr*, plural '*pr.w*. The word can be found widely distributed in the most varying places of the ancient East, under correspondingly differing conditions, from the end of the third millennium until about the twelfth century BC.[60] In view of the philological identity of the word (which is hardly open to dispute), it seemed an obvious conjecture that a more or less identical phenomenon, relating to groups of people, was to be understood. Now, it is from the outset highly improbable that we have to do here with a collective ethnic term, i.e., the name of a people, or the name of groups bound together into a tribe. It seems more likely that this was a name for people living under particular conditions, perhaps people accustomed to a nomadic or semi-nomadic life.[61] The opinion therefore came to be widely accepted that the expression ought correctly to be interpreted sociologically, and that it covered particular non-established elements, who were either still moving about or who, within established social organizations, had not yet found themselves a social organization of their own; i.e., dependent workers who were 'economic failures, deprived of their rights'.[62]

At first sight the application of the term to the Semitic elements in Egypt can then be readily understood. For they were under foreign jurisdiction, in a dependent position, excluded from the legal status of free and independent people. The term's application would therefore be quite suitable; the only remarkable thing about it is that the expression later, in other circumstances, only appears in Old Testament texts belonging to the period before the kings in connection with the Philistines, and disappears entirely from all

other oriental literature. We cannot and need not try to find the
solution of this latter problem here. But we must interpolate a consideration of a more general nature.

It is from the outset hardly probable that a term used over so
great a period of time in different places also preserved the same
range of meaning in every case. It is certainly possible that a basic
association, tending in one and the same direction, played a part in
its application; but we must equally reckon with the likelihood
that in the course of time it was also used as a handy common
denominator for different phenomena. This would demand
detailed investigation. But in any case the question remains, in
what sense an actual identity existed, or continued to exist, when
the people who were elsewhere called *ḫabiru* were termed *'pr.w* in
Egypt. Moreover, it is not even certain whether this word was
from the very beginning identical in meaning with *ḫabiru/'pr.w*. [63]
In Egypt the expression is only authenticated from the period of
the New Kingdom, and is then largely used for prisoners of war
from the neighbouring Asiatic neighbourhood (i.e., Syria and
Palestine). Thus far we really could assume a borrowing of the
term *ḫabiru*. On the other hand, however, in Egypt it is not itself
identical with 'prisoner of war' or 'slave'. It seems, rather, to lose
its socially disparaging meaning and to take on a value of its own
within the Egyptian social structure, for groups of non-Egyptian
workers with their own legal status. [64]

This indication of the term's change of nuance inside Egypt
may serve to show that *ḫabiru* need not be absolutely the same as
'pr.w, and this in its turn should warn us to be cautious about a
sweeping equation of *'ibrī* with *ḫabiru* or *'pr.w*. Thus it might
already be asked with reference to the 'Hebrews' working in the
eastern delta whether we ought to understand these people as
being 'economic failures and rootless people without rights' in the
sense of *ḫabiru*; or whether they should not be considered, in a
much more neutral sense, to be foreign workers from the Bedouin
neighbourhood employed by the Egyptians, with a legal status of
their own. According to all the factors that have been weighed up
here, the latter commends itself far more. But can we therefore
simply assume that 'Hebrews' conceals the special name *'pr.w*
which the Egyptians gave these people, i.e., that an Egyptian
'legal status' has authentically passed into the Old Testament
text? [65] Is it not more obvious to see the transfer of the term

Hebrew as being a proceeding in line with Israelite feeling, growing up out of the midst of Old Testament thinking itself, and which remained meaningful, at least for the later Israelite reader?

Klaus Koch's recent judgment does in fact point in this direction.[66] Taking the genealogies in Genesis into account, he wants to understand certain peoples who appear there as the sons of Eber (Gen. 10.21ff.) – but who are otherwise identical with the already mentioned descendants of Abraham in the framework of the genealogical system – as the 'Hebrew peoples', to whom alone the expression *'ibrī* applies. With this Koch removes the term *'ibrī* from the orbit of the *ḫabiru* problem, thereby also removing it from the field of sociological interpretation. He sees it as being the name for a people – more precisely, a name for the peoples who, in the train of the Aramaean wanderings, appear in Genesis as the kindred of Abraham, in the narrower sense (taking account of Num. 24.3–9, 15–23) Israel, Moab, Edom, Amalek and Cain. 'Hebrews' are therefore more than 'Israelites'. It is an overriding ethnic concept, an effective term for Israel and its neighbouring tribes, before Israel and beside it. As such it could then also play an independent part in I Samuel over against the Philistines, who were ethnically different. But in Egypt, where there was as yet no 'Israel' in the later sense, it could also appropriately mean the Semitic elements who, coming from the desert, spent some time there.

Though much in Koch's thesis and his development of it may remain controversial in detail, it none the less speaks in favour of a separate interpretation of the term *'ibrī*, unencumbered by *ḫabiru* and *'pr.w*; and it achieves the beginnings of an interpretation which does justice to the ethnic reality governing a part of the Aramaean migrations, independent of sociological categories and theories.

If one cautiously narrows down Koch's intentions, it can be said that the term Hebrew, which is locally and temporally limited in the Old Testament, corresponds to an overriding ethnic designation. This designation applied to a section of the tribes and peoples which, in the wake of the Aramaean movement, as land-seeking groups approached southern Syria, and especially the area of Palestine and the Sinai peninsula, from the direction of the Arabian desert. Organically this conviction would also fit the 'small-scale' solution which has been supported above for the relationship between the patriarchs and the Egyptian groups.[67]

The two stand in an immediate temporal and geographical continuity and ultimately have the same root. They are component parts of the movement from the east towards the cultivated lands of Syria and Palestine, a movement which is almost contemporary with the migration of the Sea Peoples from the west. 'Israel's' presence in Egypt presents itself in the framework of the world history of the time as part of a Semitic wave of peoples who wanted to take possession of the cultivated lands of the Fertile Crescent. What actually proved possible in Syria and Palestine came to grief in the Egyptian eastern delta, which, because of the situation of the time and the inclination of the delta's ruler, was not open to permanent possession. Thus the 'exodus' became necessary, with a new goal which was finally attained in Palestine, in association with other tribes. It is on this exodus event that the biblical account in the Pentateuch concentrates. We shall now have to say something more about its details, but above all about the leading figure in the event: Moses.

IV

THE EXODUS AND THE ROLE OF MOSES

The biblical account of the departure from Egypt given to us in the Book of Exodus must now be seen against the wide horizon of world history, with all its interactions. The biblical account (which – if we include the events at the Reed Sea – covers Ex. 1–15) is put together from a series of individual traditions which usually only have the character of single scenes. In spite of this, the intention of combining the tradition into a dramatic series of scenes is quite unmistakable. Drama, however, comes into being through people, through dialogue, through the confrontation of these persons with situations. The account therefore clusters, essentially speaking, round particular individuals. 'Hebrews' and 'Israelites' on the one side, Egyptians on the other, appear in the train of these actors only as an undifferentiated multitude in the background. They are the people who are ultimately at stake, but they do not carry the action; they form no resolves and make no decisions. They almost always subordinate themselves unconditionally to the salient characters and allow themselves to be disposed of by them.

The group which determines the course of the action is quickly described. On the Egyptian side it is solely the Pharaoh, together with some official soothsayer priests, and the Pharaoh's daughter, who finds the baby Moses after he has been exposed; the Egyptian whom Moses kills is a nameless, marginal figure. On the Israelite side, Moses appears as the absolutely outstanding personality, behind whom Aaron takes a very secondary place; all the other people only enter the scene at particular points and are subordinated to events: Moses' wife Zipporah (especially in the curious scene in Ex. 4.24–26); Moses' sister, who watches the

exposed child; the two Hebrew midwives who avoid fulfilling
Pharaoh's command to kill all the male children. Last but not
least, a person and power of his own on Israel's side is Yahweh.
We only have to add, from the Midianite side, the priest Jethro
with his daughters, one of whom Moses marries.

This concentration of events on only a very few figures is in
accordance with the lucid construction and course of the plot.
Exodus 1 is in fact simply an exposition, where we find in concentrated form the themes which form the preconditions for the
events that follow. The sons of Jacob have grown into a great
people in Egypt. The Pharaoh who knew Joseph is no longer
living. The increasing growth of the Israelite population makes the
Egyptians fear that their superior strength could be a danger if
they were to fight on the side of Egypt's enemies. The Egyptian
counter-measure (a not entirely convincing one) is the employment of the Israelites in the building of the 'store cities' Pithom
and Ramesses. This measure does not prevent their growth at all,
and indeed encourages it. But the hard labour does at least em-
bitter the Israelites. Finally, however, no way out is left to the
Egyptian king except the deliberate extermination of the rising
Hebrew generation. Two Hebrew midwives are appointed to see
to it that no male child remains alive. The godly fear of these
women prevents them from carrying out the Pharaoh's command.
Finally the general command goes forth that newly born Hebrew
children are to be thrown into the Nile.

Factually speaking, this is all we are directly told about the time
spent by the Israelites in Egypt; it is an entirely pragmatic selection
of details designed to prepare us for what is to come. Moreover,
the infanticide motif already belongs, strictly speaking, to the
following story of the birth and exposure of Moses – the man who
moves into the centre of interest from Ex. 2 onwards. Moses, the
liberator of his people from Egyptian oppression, was himself
threatened from his earliest days. Exposed as a child, he was found
and saved, and later persecuted in his fight for justice for his fellow
countrymen. He flees, and outside Egypt, in the nearby Midianite
countryside, not only meets his wife but also encounters the strange
and yet familiar God who presents himself as the God of his
fathers. This God appears to Moses in the lonely steppe country
and speaks to him out of a burning thorn bush. Moses is given the
commission to lead his oppressed countrymen out of Egypt and to

bring them to a land flowing with milk and honey. After some
hesitation Moses returns to Egypt because the king who wanted to
kill him is no longer alive. But the carrying out of the divine commission proves to be exceedingly difficult. Together with Aaron,
Moses enters on negotiations with the Pharaoh. The pretext that
the people want to withdraw to the desert for a pilgrimage and
feast avails nothing with the king. He does not know 'the God of
the Hebrews' and owes him no obedience. The people are not
allowed to rest, working conditions being expressly tightened up.
Moses despairs. God himself must intervene through signs and
miracles and force the Egyptian king to give in. It is highly
peculiar, it may be noted, that the Pharaoh, once the most un-
yielding antagonist of the Hebrew people who have grown so
mighty in his country, does not immediately send them away but
keeps them in the country almost by force. None of plagues which
now descend on Egypt, severe though they are, alters this. It is
only at the very end, when Egypt's firstborn are struck, that the
king opens up the way. But he regrets his decision once more and
chases after the departing Israelites, though without success. At
the Reed Sea the pursuers suffer a crushing defeat. Now the way to
freedom is open to the people – the way to the promised land.

A closer glance reveals tensions and certain contradictions in
the apparently smooth course of the plot. The inconsistency in the
behaviour of the Egyptian king, who first wants to destroy the
Israelite people in his own country, but who is later not prepared
to let them leave it, is not only due to the fact that this was
apparently not one and the same king; different kinds of approach
also play a part. On the one hand the king is presented as violently
brutal, on the other hand as being an obdurate despot, who in
every event only wishes the Hebrew people ill, not only thinking
of exterminating them but also disregarding their wishes. But
these nuances of motive, which can be observed even more frequently, are connected with the employment of different literary
units, which again have their own individual origins and pursue
independent tendencies within themselves. Thus, for example, in
Ex. 3 the revelation of Yahweh at the burning bush is greatly
expanded, and is enriched by the scene of enquiry about the divine
name, which also raises the episode to independent theological
importance. It is later apparently supplemented by a somewhat
different version of the divine self-revelation (Ex. 6.2ff.). But here

we have an entirely different kind of account. No less independent is the accumulation of plagues, whose peak, the slaying of Egypt's firstborn, not only causes the king to allow the exodus but at the same time provides the reason for the passover rite. Here, within the happening, with its unmistakable pragmatism, particular theological accents are set and traditions are assimilated which had been handed down as being associated with Moses and the exodus.

It has long been recognized that the literary stratification of the source fragments in the Book of Exodus follows principles which are common to the whole Pentateuch. In the Book of Exodus, too, we can observe the three source strata which scholarly convention knows as the Yahwist, the Elohist and the Priestly document. It is to these that the differing tendencies in the course of the account are very largely due. We shall have to say more about this at a later point. At the moment we are simply concerned to establish that the account of Israel's presence in Egypt and the exodus must not be judged as an objective record, but follows independent principles and interests which are only in part suitable for use in an exact historical evaluation. Methodologically, therefore, we must distinguish between the historical background, which we have built up by other means, and the Israelite view of the event, which finds expression in the Book of Exodus. This does not eliminate the reliability of historical reminiscence in individual cases, as for example the mention of the cities of Pithom and Ramesses, the Midianite region and the mountain of God. But the question, of course, remains: what part was actually played by the personalities who are moved into the centre of events? How far, that is to say, does the Old Testament text correspond, at least approximately, to historical fact in its description of these persons?

First, as far as the figure of the Pharaoh is concerned: it is absolutely stereotyped, without any individual features; his name is nowhere mentioned in the Book of Exodus. Whether on the other hand Aaron, who was an essential key figure for the Israelite priesthood, originally played any part at all in the Exodus event is highly problematical. Perhaps he was designed to be artificially approximated to the figure of Moses (as happens in a not very convincing way when he becomes Moses' spokesman in Ex. 4.10–17). The question has to be investigated in the wider context of the traditions of the ancient Israelite priesthood.[1] Thus we are left ultimately with only the mighty figure of Moses, which cannot be put aside as invention or interpolation, but which is constitutive for the whole account. Who, then, was Moses? And how is it possible to make this man's existence and function as plausible as possible through the methods of historical research?

Moses' range of function seems to be unusual. It is he who receives the revelation of the God Yahweh; it is he who is charged with the commission to bring the people out of Egypt and who himself leads his people, overcoming all difficulties; again, it is he who receives the Law and its precepts on the mountain of God, and who, in an almost priestly capacity, mediates between Yahweh and the people; it is he who himself approaches almost to the promised land but, in a positively tragic heightening of the event, dies in the very face of his lifetime's goal. It is not surprising that this obviously fascinating figure was varyingly interpreted and judged in the course of time, and that in each case certain individual features of his nature and work were used to classify the man more closely. Thus he could be understood on the model of other Israelite offices and functions, as prophet, priest or judge – indeed even as the holder of a 'Mosaic office' deriving from him; or attempts were made to do him justice by comparing him with other phenomena in the history of religion, terming him the founder of a religion, a reformer, a theologian, the establisher of an order and a nation. He is even supposed to have acted as a 'sorcerer'. Nor have attempts been lacking to compare or identify him with gods and to turn him into a mythological figure.[2] Some of these classifications may indeed contain grains of truth; but none the less they can contribute little to a convincing proof of Moses' historicity. Consequently modern research into Moses[3] has deliberately aimed at restricting the original radius of Moses' activity in order to come closer to the real root of his personality.

In connection with the problems of literary criticism presented by the Pentateuch, Noth's approach[4] has had a particularly stimulating as well as a provocative effect. Noth split up the Pentateuch material into a series of general themes and then asked to which of the themes Moses originally belonged. Admittedly, he finally arrived at the conclusion that Moses was not really anchored in any one of these themes: he belonged neither in the 'deliverance from Egypt', nor in the 'bringing into the cultivated lands of Palestine', nor yet in the 'promise to the patriarchs' or the 'leading in the wilderness' – indeed not even in the 'revelation on Sinai'. The only thing of which we can be certain, according to Noth, is the tradition that his grave lay in Transjordania. But, he maintains, literary developments or, more precisely, the history of tradition, gradually grafted Moses into the different themes and turned him into a figure which bound them together, forming a convincing link between the individual complexes of the tradition.

Here we cannot even try to investigate and evaluate the details of these postulates and their reasonably justifiable points of departure.[5] That they were bound to evoke contradiction is obvious; and indeed it must be said that solutions in so complicated a field of literary and historical research are not easily come by, and have not yet been adequately arrived at even today. Part of the discussion has concentrated on nevertheless assigning Moses to one or to several of the Pentateuch themes, in contrast to Noth; here, understandably, the themes of 'the deliverance from Egypt' and 'the revelation on Sinai' are bound to appear on the short list. For in these the function of Moses seems to be positively indispensable. But the other way ought not to be excluded either: that is to say, to leave Moses within all the themes of the Pentateuch, in spite of the understandable objections, on the basis of the reflection that a single individual could certainly have been involved in a series of wanderings between Egypt and Palestine, however involved the details of the individual event may have been. This single event could later have been expanded in the Pentateuch through the enrichment of additional traditions, so that to our eyes the whole happening seems more tremendous than it may probably have been in its historical essence. Even in the case of Moses, we should not therefore reckon with vast areas of time but with a temporally and geographically limited sphere of action. The most important thing of all, however, is to find if possible some points of departure, unique in their very nature, which cannot have been invented and which may enable us to find a firm basis, independent of literary expansions, for the historical setting of Moses.

It would probably be correct to see the first starting point of this kind as being the name Moses itself. The most convincing interpretation is still that it contains a common Egyptian name element, such as reappears most clearly in a name like 'Thutmosis'. The structure of many Egyptian names is based on the juxtaposition of the name of a god and the root *mśy*, to give birth to, so

that they might be translated as 'the god . . . is born' or 'the god
. . . has given birth (to him)'. [6] Now, in the name Moses the
name of the god seems to have been broken off, only the element
characterized by *mśy* remaining, so that it has become a shortened
name – for which there is also occasional Egyptian evidence. [7]

But if Moses bore an Egyptian name, it is legitimate to assume
that he himself had contact with Egypt, [8] and was either given the
name there as a mere nickname [9] or came to possess it in a quite
legitimate way. As the son of Semitic parents, he could as a child
undoubtedly have already been in the Egyptian service, or – even
more probably – could have been the child of Semites who were
themselves in the Egyptian service, the children of such people
frequently being given Egyptian names. We possess documents
confirming this legal practice from as early as the period of the
Middle Kingdom; these documents contain the lists of Semitic
workers (together with their children) who worked for Egyptians
in prominent positions. The most interesting and detailed document of this kind found up to now dates from the thirteenth
dynasty and is a list drawn up on papyrus of 95 people, both
natives and 48 'Asiatics', who were probably all in the service of a
woman called Senebtisi. [10] The 'Asiatics' are in fact Semites who
had immigrated and entered the service of this high-ranking
Egyptian lady. The list is divided into columns. First the servant's
name is mentioned (male or female). In the second column stands
the word 'called . . .', followed by the name given to the person
in question in Egypt, probably because it was harder to remember
the foreign name, and the Egyptian one was at all events easier.
The third column lists the work done by the person; and the
fourth the sex. An interesting case is, for example, the 'Asiatic'
woman *Bʿȝtwj*, [11] who was called *Wȝḥ-rś-śnb* in Egypt and whose
little daughter has an entry of her own. We read: 'Her daughter
Senebtisi, that is her (original) name; child.' [12] An occupation is
understandably not given; her mother was put down as 'worker'.
Senebtisi was very probably only born in the Egyptian house and
was given the name of the mistress whom her mother served.

This case throws light on Moses, too, even if he lived a number
of centuries later than the papyrus we have drawn on here. Circumstances would have altered little, basically speaking. It can be
seen in what circumstances a person could acquire an Egyptian
name in a quite regular way, either by being renamed in Egypt, or

because he was already given the name from the beginning, as a child born there. We do not need to go into detail here about the precise degree of vassalage into which Semites in Egypt could enter, with or without Egyptian names. Conditions are confirmed and supplemented by other sources, apart from the papyrus mentioned here, for example stele inscriptions.[13] It is easily conceivable that the relationship between individual Egyptians and the Semites bound to them was a close one and that it was consequently possible for cases to occur in actual fact which are only known to us in the form of literary themes. This applies to the attempt to seduce the dependent foreigner,[14] known to us under the heading of Potiphar's wife; but it is equally true of the story of the exposure of the baby Moses in the bulrushes,[15] which ends with the Pharaoh's daughter adopting the foundling in place of a son and giving him a name.[16] This cannot be used as proof of the literal historicity of the bulrushes story, nor is it intended to be such; yet in the motif of adoption and naming there is an accurate element illustrating the way in which Semitic children could to some extent be integrated into Egyptian society. For the rest, it can hardly be disputed that the main emphasis of this story lies in the miraculous deliverance of the hero endangered in his earliest youth – a favourite motif in ancient sagas, now transferred to Moses.[17]

Moses can therefore have received his name in the Egyptian service, whether he himself entered that service or whether he was born of Semitic parents who belonged to it. There is no foundation for believing that Moses himself was an Egyptian. On the contrary, he stood up for his 'brothers',[18] killing an Egyptian who had beaten a Hebrew worker. When he found that the murder was public knowledge, he fled the country, met the Midianites and their high priest Jethro, and entered his service. As he pastured Jethro's flock, he came upon a remote mountain country where he received the divine revelation which later caused him to return to Egypt.[19]

The flight into Midian beyond the east delta border is a faint reminiscence of the flight of Sinuhe, who saved himself from investigation in the same way.[20] Like Sinuhe, Moses too soon comes upon a desert tribe which receives him in friendly fashion. For all that, some scholars have wanted to call Moses' escape into Midian in question, less for historical reasons than for reasons

connected with the history of the tradition.[21] That the Midianite
area was the scene of Moses' first encounter with God was a primary
datum, it is claimed. Moses therefore had to arrive at that particular place in order to receive the commission for the exodus. As
long as he was confined to Egypt, he would have had no opportunity, practically speaking, to come to know the God of the
exodus. This compulsion, deriving from historical-theological
criteria, produced the early encounter of Moses with this God,
which can in reality only have taken place later in Moses' life.

Since these questions can in any case only be solved hypothetic-
ally, we may here add the additional hypothesis that the Semitic
elements in Egypt, among which Moses could number himself,
had already encountered this God of the mountain in the Midianite
region before their entry into Egypt. How else can one explain
their wish to go three days into the wilderness to prepare a feast
for their God, unless one chooses to see these words as a mere
manoeuvre to deceive Pharaoh?[22] Since, however, the Book of
Exodus says nothing about the immediately foregoing history of
the 'Hebrews' who were in Egypt, and apparently knows nothing
about it, knowledge of the God of the exodus had to be established
before the exodus itself. This is stressed in the case of Moses in the
incident of the burning bush, which belongs within the context
of his stay in Midian. Thus far, this stay need not necessarily have
been originally connected with the experiences at the Mountain of
God; but the two complexes are closely related, factually and
locally, and there is therefore no need to interpret them as being
purely contradictory, either.[23]

These considerations may serve to show that it is really not easy
to write a continuous story of Moses – if indeed it is not impossible.
The information we have about him is harnessed to the concerns
of the Exodus account, which is purposefully directed towards
letting the future saviour of Israel experience his divine revelation
as early as possible. Consequently, individual traditions are treated
with a high hand; and what was historically more complicated,
and is in detail no longer accessible to us today, may actually have
been simplified for the sake of the exposition of the exodus event.
Moses' dispute with the Pharaoh and the plagues which finally
break out are beyond all the checks open to us; they were in-
corporated here for reasons which we shall have to discuss in connection with the passover. At all events, Moses succeeds in

preparing the exodus and in finally carrying it through success-fully. This leads us to define the historical role of Moses at the exodus as that of a man who, in the desperate situation which faced the Bedouins who had penetrated the eastern delta, weighed down by the building activities of the Egyptians, took the initiative and prepared, organized and led their departure – if indeed it was not a hasty flight. For this Moses may have been particularly qualified, but also particularly favoured. He may have been longer in the country and perhaps had contact with government officials – or so we may suppose if we want to scale down the dispute with the Pharaoh to credible proportions. He would certainly have possessed a clear picture of the escape routes and the most favour-able times for departure; here he may even have exploited the trust of Egyptian officials. We cannot know any of these things, but it lies within the realm of the possible, and can be easily reconstructed from what we were able to piece together about the frontier traffic in the eastern delta. In certain circumstances, one good contact with an officer of the frontier force (like the one we met in the frontier official's report)[24] would have been enough to make the departure feasible and to secure it.

The other way of handling the history of the tradition is to allow Moses to play a part only on the mountain of God and to maintain that it was only at a later stage, through literary develop-ment, that he grew into the exodus, as its successful leader. But this seems much more difficult to imagine. Certainly it may be possible to reconstruct the exodus event without Moses, perhaps by postulating that the oppressed Israelites attempted to break out by themselves. But is it really permissible to encumber transmitted material by eliminating dominating elements, so that the under-standing of the whole is not furthered, but rather made more difficult? After all, in this case one would have to explain in detail how Moses could still become the essential key figure of the exodus. We do not have to deal here with the role of Moses during the journey through the wilderness; but we may just add – follow-ing up this approach – that the Moses who launched the exodus was sufficiently qualified to take over the further leadership of his group and to grow into those functions which were demanded of him by the happening on the mountain of God. That he himself finally failed to enter the promised land can hardly be an invention. He really must have died beforehand.

The presuppositions for this sketch of the historical functions
of Moses rest – let me stress once more – on the assumption that
the course of events outlined in the Pentateuch from the Book of
Exodus to the Book of Numbers covers hardly more than the
space of a single generation. The foregoing history was undoubtedly longer and more complicated. But from the Exodus
down to the beginning of the occupation of Palestine we cannot
assume any extraordinarily extensive span of time – also taking
into account the later history of Israel. Moreover, this more or
less corresponds to the biblical view, which in some of its traditions puts the wanderings in the desert at forty years.[25]

These chronological considerations should finally be supplemented by some further figures which we have in connection with
Israel's stay in Egypt. They are unfortunately contradictory among
themselves. According to Ex. 12.40f. the sojourn lasted 430 years,
but according to Gen. 15.13 it was 400 years. In a quite different
passage – I Kings 6.1 – we are told that Solomon began to build
the temple in the fourth year of his reign, and that this was the
480th year after the exodus from Egypt. Some other figures are
considerably lower. According to Gen. 15.16 Abraham is told
that the fourth generation might already return to Palestine.
Similarly, Ex. 6.13ff. reckons with four generations from the sons
of Jacob until Moses. This period of four generations can hardly
be estimated at more than 120 years. The Septuagint is different
again; it relates the 430 years of Ex. 12.40f. to Israel's dwelling 'in
the land of Egypt and in the land of Canaan'[26], and in I Kings 6.1
has only 440 years for the 480 between the exodus and the building
of the temple.

These highly differing statements do not encourage us to
attempt to discover the possibly correct figure by way of all kinds
of combinations and computations. It is more justifiable to enquire
how the figures ever came into existence. In each case they belong
in the biblical books to a particular system of reference which is
designed to secure a relative chronology within the Old Testament
historical accounts that is as well balanced as possible. This is
clearest in the case of the 480 years between the exodus and the
building of the temple, which is intended to cover an era of twelve
times forty years, i.e., probably twelve generations. It is possible
to show that the other numbers mentioned within the Deuteronomic History[27] are so ordered and matched against one another

that in the end we more or less arrive at this figure of 480. [28] Moreover, it must be remembered that historical figures and the division of history into periods do not, in the biblical writings, primarily serve an exclusively annalistic end in itself; but that through the conscious choice of a number, especially in the case of round numbers, a theological statement can also be intended, in addition to the purely chronological one. In the rounding off of the eras and the balancing out of their duration, the God who governs history is to be experienced and confirmed as the purposeful shaper of events.

Unfortunately, the trend of the system of numbers in the Priestly stratum of the Pentateuch is not so transparent as that of the Deuteronomic history; but its numbers, too, must be understood as being moulded by the compulsion of a more overriding system. This system begins impressively in Gen. 5 with the succession of generations from the beginning of man down to Noah (which is intended to be a chronology); and it is within this framework that 430 years are stated to be the length of Israel's stay in Egypt. The note about the 400 years in Gen. 15.13 ought probably to be considered as a rounding off of these 430 years. We might also ask whether the idea of the four generations, which exists parallel to this, is a reduction starting from the 400 years; but this cannot be proved. At all events, a shorter period of time was obviously reckoned to have elapsed between the patriarchs and Moses.

The large number of 400 and more years is sometimes drawn on by those scholars who would like to connect the emergence in Egypt of what were later Israelites with the Hyksos. If the exodus is assigned to the thirteenth century BC, and if the 400 years are taken into account, one does actually arrive at the period of the decline of the Egyptian kingdom, and hence at the Hyksos period. But other weighty reasons speak against this assumption – reasons which can scarcely lose their force because of numerical statements in the Bible, which for their own part are not consistently attested. [29] After all, according to our knowledge, the 480 years between the exodus and the building of the temple are not correct either. The figure given is undoubtedly too high. The exodus would then fall roughly in the period of Amenophis IV, Akhenaten, which is quite improbable. That Ramesses II was the Pharaoh of the oppression may with justice be concluded from the mention

of the city of Ramesses; and this also stands in an acceptable relationship to the further course of Israel's history. Because Ex. 2.23
mentions the death of the king of the oppression, the conclusion
has been drawn that the exodus took place under Ramesses II's
successor, King Merneptah (*c.* 1223–1203). This is not entirely out
of the question, even though it is not absolutely required on the
basis of Ex. 2.23. There are, on the other hand, no compelling
reasons against the view that the exodus already took place under
Ramesses II. [30]

The biblical information about numbers of years has its own
tendencies and viewpoints, just as happens with the biblical
accounts in general. These inevitably lead to certain discrepancies
between our modern historical knowledge and the particular
narrative method of ancient traditions. This has been shown here
in connection with the basic conception of Ex. 1–15, and especially
with the interpretation of Moses. The exodus account has, moreover, a number of special passages in which its own theological
interest comes to the fore more strongly than elsewhere. We have
still to look very briefly at these passages (which determine the
exodus account to no small degree) before we can pass final judgment on Israel's stay in Egypt and the biblical account of it.

V

THE FORMATION OF THE TRADITION AND ITS LONG-TERM HISTORICAL EFFECTS

We have already stressed several times that the various source units used in the Book of Exodus owe their origin to different periods, and that they were finally put together in order to trace out a dramatic course of events which should be convincing as a whole. This course of events has its own highlights, which are not only grounded in the character of what took place as pure event, but which bring out the meaning that these events also had for the future. The appearance of God at the burning bush is a highlight of this kind, one which is simultaneously linked up with an explanatory proclamation of the divine name. The plagues represent a block of their own, which ends with the institution of the passover for Israel. The last extensively developed climax in connection with the exodus is the happening at the Reed Sea, which – adorned with miraculous features – is not only described but also sung. It is not chance that later strata of tradition especially play a part in these sections, and that here event and interpretation are already particularly closely entwined.

Because the exodus event became of constitutive significance for Israel's consciousness, individual elements in its course took on a heightened interest, and consequently were also the object of more insistent reflection. It is under this aspect of the formation and the processing of tradition that we shall be briefly considering the three fragments touched on here.

(a) The divine appearance and the divine name

The story of the appearance of God at the burning bush is a composition which is complicated in its details;[1] but it has as its main point the commission to Moses to lead the oppressed Israelites out of Egypt. It is very closely connected with God's presentation of himself, though he conceals his proper name, Yahweh, throughout and merely declares that he is the God of the fathers, the God of Abraham, Isaac and Jacob. It is only when Moses expressly asks what he should say when the Israelites ask the name of the God who sent him, that God gives the information which is usually represented by the words, 'I am who I am', and goes on: 'Say this to the people of Israel, "I AM has sent me to you".'[2] This Hebrew form *'ehyeh*, translated by 'I am', is always understood as being a play on the name of God, Yahweh, which appears here in veiled form, but which is probably supposed, especially in this form, to be interpreted in a particular way. Now, it is true that an exact etymological explanation of the divine name Yahweh, which has been repeatedly attempted from the Semitic side, has remained an unsolved problem down to the present day.[3] Purely formally, the name is put together from the root *hwh*, to which a preceding *y* has been added. In this way it can certainly be assigned to the group of those western Semitic short-name formations which we have already observed in some of the names belonging to the patriarchs. An unequivocal[4] translation of the root *hwh* is admittedly impossible. Even the Hebrew attempt in Ex. 3.14 to come nearer to an interpretation with the help of the root *hyh*, 'to be', can only be judged as 'popular etymology', and by no means offers an authentic philological explanation.

However, for the understanding of God's naming of himself in Ex. 3.14 an interpretation of the name Yahweh that can hold its ground against the standards of modern philology is not so important. It is more essential to discover what the biblical writer meant when he put this singular 'I am who I am' into the mouth of God as an answer to Moses' question about the divine name, associating it at the same time with the indication that this God concealed behind the 'I am' was the God of the fathers, the God of Abraham, Isaac and Jacob. There is no doubt at all that at this decisive point, when God talks with Moses for the first time, this God is the subject of a particular kind of reflection. Of course this is not to be taken in the sense (common in later interpretations of the introductory formula) that in the 'I am' this God is manifesting himself as the Eternal Being, or as the one who is eternally and unchangeably active in an ontic category;

but this is reflection of a highly remarkable historical and theological kind. Its purpose is to establish the identity – or, to be more exact, the historical continuity – of experiences of the divine which exists between the faith of the patriarchs and the God who manifests himself to Moses. For it is the God of Israel who appeared to the patriarchs and who will now guarantee the exodus. Whatever the name of this God may be, he is the one who is active in history and in the present. The 'I am who I am' must not, therefore, be detached from its present context, as if it were an isolated attempt to find an explanation for the name of God; the process is the reverse one: the 'I am' is also to be understood out of the situation that is presented here, as an expression of the determination of the God who is appearing here, the God who presents himself as the God of the fathers, and who is prepared really to will this exodus and to support it by every possible means. This 'I am who I am' is an expression of a heightened solemnity and fervour on the part of the deity, who is determined to complete what he has once planned.

In confirmation of this interpretation, Alt pointed years ago to the passage in the historical section of the *Instruction for Merikare* where the king solemnly introduces the description of his countermeasures against the thieving Bedouins with the formula, 'But as I live! I am while I am!', thus expressing his determination.[5] There is, of course, no suggestion here that the passage Ex. 3.14 is directly dependent on the Egyptian text, but, as Alt says, we no doubt have to do 'in both cases with the same kind of expression for the speaker's extremely heightened consciousness of his own being and his own power'.[6] Thus in the use of this formula[7] the particular topical utterance of the divine determination which is demanded by the context is joined with an etymological play on the name of God. This view of the passage has the advantage of freeing the interpretation of the 'I am' from all possible speculations about Being, and of supporting a dynamic conception which is in accord with the God of Israel and his constant presence in the course of a continually mutable flow of events.[8] In many respects the author of Ex. 3 has in this way achieved his goal. He has localized the appearance of God which Moses experienced at the mountain of God in the Midianite area; he has defined that God as the God of Israel – as the God who has been continuously present and active since the days of the patriarchs, and who is now

determined to intervene in a situation of acute need and to bring
to bear his whole historically effective power, which is summed up
in the fervent 'I am'. For this is the God with whom Moses has to
do when he now approaches the heavy task of leading the people
out of the country; it is Yahweh, whose name is communicated in
hidden form in the etymologizing *'ehyeh*.

It must be clear that here, in Ex. 3.13–15, more is being offered
than a mere pragmatic historical account; at the same time, at a
culminating point in the event, we are given an equally momentous
historical and theological interpretation of these happenings, which
actually leads to a grasp of the nature of the Godhead. In this way
this first example shows how in the course of later reflective work
on the exodus tradition the event was deepened and saturated with
thought. For the bond between the religion of the patriarchs and
belief in Yahweh, which Ex. 3 sets out to underline, also after all
presupposes an advanced stage in the formation of Israelite tradition, in which the patriarchal tradition and the tradition about
Egypt were understood as being components of the future Israel.
Through Ex. 3 these components find their theological legitimation for Israel's existence in the scene of the divine appearance.
The God of the fathers and Yahweh are one.

(b) Plagues and passover

Exodus 7.8–10.29 describes with unusual expansiveness (within
the framework of a stereotyped scheme) nine plagues, which have
mainly the character of swarms of vermin and insect pests, violent
storms, and sickness. [9] These are followed (Ex. 11f.) by the last and
most momentous plague, the extermination of the Egyptian firstborn. The plagues are the result of the Egyptian king's obstinate
attitude towards Moses; he continually refuses to allow the people
to leave, and remains unsoftened even by the most frightful catas-
trophes of nature. Every new stubbornness on the part of the
Pharaoh releases a new plague. Noth[10] has pointed out that in the
stereotyped account, which could have been extended at will, two
formulae occur side by side; on the one hand, 'Pharaoh hardened
his heart' and on the other, 'Yahweh hardened Pharaoh's heart'.
The two formulae are used indiscriminately, but the second finally
predominates. Here a tendency emerges which remained important for the later tradition about the sojourn in Egypt as well.
Yahweh showed himself as mighty to the Egyptians through great

signs and wonders;[11] he positively saw to it that Pharaoh hardened his heart against Moses' wishes. In this way he had the opportunity of displaying his power through new plagues which he increasingly visited on the Egyptians, as the oppressors of Israel.

Of course this is not the only motif of the plague complex, although it finds some sort of climax at the end of Ex. 10. In fact the series of plagues is directed towards a final climax, which finds expression in the extermination of the Egyptian firstborn, and finally persuades the Pharaoh to change his mind. We are occasionally told[12] that the Israelites were immune from all the various plagues, but in the case of the last plague this is definitely ensured through an apotropaic blood ritual. The Israelites carry out the slaughter of a suitable sacrificial animal and smear the doorposts with its blood. In this way they ward off from their houses the 'destroyer'[13] who goes round by night and slays the Egyptian firstborn. In this way Yahweh will 'spare' the Israelites, he will 'pass over' them. These are hypothetical translations of the verb *psḥ*, which is the basis of the Hebrew word *pesaḥ*. The sacrifice is therefore designed to ensure a 'sparing', a 'passing over', in which the apotropaic character of the action is at least touched on.

One must, of course, ask whether this is the original meaning of the passover (*pesaḥ*) – whether it really corresponds to the exodus situation in the way described in Ex. 12. It has rightly been pointed out[14] that the *pesaḥ* conceals an older rite, a rite which may even be older than the exodus. The sacrifice of the firstborn of the sheep or goats belonged most probably to the immemorial customs of the nomadic herdsmen of these smaller beasts. When the change was made from winter to summer pastures and before the dangers of the hot summer season, the sacrifice was thought to be a way of warding off evil powers. This, too, was an apotropaic rite, though it was not designed to ward off a single, acute danger, but to meet the perils which cropped up periodically in the rhythm of the seasons. In the case of the passover in Ex. 12, this Bedouin sacrificial custom found a unique historical explanation; it was given a historical basis through a particular event in the history of Israel. It is directly bound up as closely as possible with God's saving action on behalf of Israel in Egypt, and is aetiologically anchored in that act. The Israelites are to eat of this sacrifice in great haste, already equipped for the start; and nothing is to be left over. This is highly understandable in the light of the exodus situation, but it is probably also an even older element in the tradition, which reflects the departure for summer pastures.

The meal of unleavened bread, the so-called *mazzoth*, is closely associated with the passover sacrifice. *Mazzoth* were round flat cakes of hastily baked bread, which were prepared on hot stones or glowing ashes. Whether, however, this meal of unleavened bread belonged from the very beginning to the meal of the passover sacrifice is not certain. It has been suggested that this is an analogy to the Bedouin custom of sacrificing from the firstborn of the cattle; and that here we have signs of an old agricultural festal tradition whose origins go back to the cultivated lands. The offering of the first-fruits of the harvest belonged to the cultic observances of the farming people and was an agricultural festival. It is noticeable that in the ancient regulations for the observance of the feast in the Book of the Covenant in Ex. 23.15, only the meal of unleavened bread appears as the first feast of the year. It is only in the later Deuteronomic Law (Deut. 16.1–8) and the Holiness Code (Lev. 23.5–8), and not least in Ex. 12 (which probably derives from the Priestly document), that the meal of unleavened bread is associated with the passover sacrifice. This may lend support to the thesis of the original independence of the two festal customs. But it is now clear that passover and unleavened bread have been at the same time historicized through the exodus situation, and that the sacred act of the exodus could thereby also shape the legend about the first Israelite feast of the year, the passover, in association with the seven-day eating of the unleavened bread. The process of the growth of the tradition is obvious. The exodus event offers the historical background, indeed even the actual occasion – the aetiology – for the two festal customs of the Bedouins and the country's farmers and peasants. It is this exodus event which provides at once the reason for these cultic customs and gives them their continuing legitimation. At the feast of the passover, the exodus, with its special circumstances and Yahweh's triumph over the Pharaoh's obduracy become the subject of a remembrance which is cultically realized in the present. The plague motif serves to prepare the passover event and therefore also belongs within the legend of the feast; it becomes its liturgical and dramatic introduction.

(c) The happenings at the Reed Sea

The events at the Reed Sea, generally known as the crossing of the

(Red) Sea, are strictly speaking already outside the period in Egypt and the exodus. But a primaeval memory of the exodus may well have been preserved in connection with this event. After all, it was only after the Reed Sea had been passed that the exodus was at last successfully achieved; consequently these events are really the organic conclusion to the Egyptian period.

Exodus 14 and 15 report what happened at the Reed Sea. For the evaluation of the details, the prose report given in Ex. 14 provides the most material. It clearly came into being by the working into a whole of different source strata, whose elements can be distinguished from one another with surprising clarity.[15] These versions are obviously presupposed in the Song of Moses and the Israelites that follows (Ex. 15.1–18); this (for reasons of form and content) is later in date, but its first verse is determined thematically by the earliest and shortest testimony, the brief hymn in 15.21 which Miriam sings:

> Sing to Yahweh, for he has triumphed gloriously;
> the horse and his rider he has thrown into the sea.

This early version of the Miriam song is probably the oldest fragment within the whole exodus tradition. It celebrates Yahweh as the real victor of the day, and is a song of triumph and praise to Yahweh alone.

At the same time it must be admitted that any direct connection with the exodus and the Reed Sea is lacking in these brief hymnic lines. But it would none the less be hard to say what better occasion there could have been for the song. The author of the Book of Exodus may therefore have been right in associating it with the Reed Sea events. These events are described in considerable detail in Ex. 14, but not without contradiction. The different statements can be largely distributed between the three Pentateuch sources of the Yahwist, the Elohist and the Priestly document, after which, in each respective case, they give a useful and, up to a certain point, a finished picture.

According to the Yahwist account, Pharaoh was sorry that he had let the Israelites go and consequently ordered the pursuit. In the face of the threat, Moses tells his people to look for a miracle, which Yahweh will perform. Both camps – the Egyptian and the Israelite – are divided from one another by pillars of cloud and of fire. Then an east wind dries out the nearby sea, and at the same time a panic arises in the Egyptian camp – a general confusion brought about by God. The Egyptians flee blindly into the area where the sea has dried out, but are swallowed up when the waters meanwhile return to their usual place; their bodies lie on the shore, as Miriam's song of victory describes: the horse and his rider he has thrown into the sea.

According to this account, therefore, the purpose of the sea is to drown the Egyptians. That it was also a definite hindrance to the Israelites on their way is not expressly stated. In this chapter it is the Yahwist account which forms the basis of the tradition. It is enriched by certain other elements, which in part motivate and explain the events differently, and represent the Elohist source stratum. The Pharaoh is told that the Israelites have fled. This causes him to follow them. In view of the Egyptian threat the Israelites have begun to waver, but we are told that they stand under the protection of the angel of God. Finally, the story goes, the chariot wheels of the pursuers were clogged and they were therefore prevented from reaching their goal. The Elohist therefore adds a few extra fragments of tradition, which, however, still allow a recognizably independent conception of the event to emerge.

The chapter's remaining textual constituent (which may be termed the Priestly account) makes a more self-contained impression. The Pharaoh is again obdurate, as he was at the end of every plague; he therefore pursues the people who have set out. The Israelites then cry to Yahweh. Yahweh commands them to set off immediately and to march through the sea. Moses stretches out his staff. The sea divides and stands in walls, and the Israelites pass between them. But as the pursuing Egyptians follow them into the sea bed, the water returns and swallows them up.

In Ex. 14 these three versions have been worked up into a single account, but they have not been so closely harmonized that it is impossible to recognize and crystallize out the different kinds of ideas as independent traditions. The details of the great event were differently related and the miracle itself was variously interpreted. One detail, even, has not been absorbed into Ex. 14 at all. We are certainly told that a pillar of cloud and fire divided the two camps; but in Josh. 24.7 we read that darkness descended between the Israelites and the Egyptians, and that the Egyptians were then covered by the sea. Both accounts presuppose that the Egyptians were as if stricken with blindness and rushed to their own doom. It is obvious that in the course of time the miraculous features became increasingly exaggerated. They advance from the drying out of the sea, via the clogged wheels of the pursuing chariots, to the damming up of the sea, which stands in walls, forming a path for the people. The difficulty is to sift what is historically reliable out of these traditions. This is not easy. One must attach considerable importance, however, to the observation in Ex. 14.5, where we are told that the Israelites had 'fled'. For the Pharaoh had allegedly given official permission for the exodus. The observation about the flight is therefore quite unmotivated and isolated, and suggests the conclusion that the idea of flight was an equally legitimate concept of Israelite tradition, which has just not become dominant in the Book of Exodus, but which has great historical probability in its favour and ultimately also provides a reason for the follow up by the Pharaoh's troops. For the rest, it must be noted that the sea brought about the Egyptians' real downfall, whether because it partly dried out or, as the Priestly document would have it, was dammed up; thus P is the only source which maintains that there was an actual 'passage' through the sea. The older tradition only tells of the perishing of the Egyptians at or in the sea, without postulating that the Israelites were in actual contact with the sea at all.

It has therefore been assumed, not unjustly, that the strange events at the 'Reed Sea' are connected with the curious character of local conditions. In the area in question the Egyptians could in actual fact have been literally surprised by the sea. Such a surprise factor shows clearly through the account in Ex. 14, even though every individual event is elaborated in miraculous terms. But to fix the place of the sea miracle is a difficult problem in itself. The assumption that the place in question is an offshoot of the Red Sea presupposes that the Israelites, after passing the eastern delta frontier, turned sharply southwards, and thereby avoided following the routes which the Bedouins were accustomed to take into the Sinai peninsula. But why should they have done this? We need not consider here another possibility that has been raised, and which seems quite exaggerated – namely that the events took place at the Gulf of Aqaba, i.e., actually beyond the Sinai peninsula.[16] Unfortunately the name 'Reed Sea', which is frequently used in the Old Testament, does not take us any further, because it is impossible to say that this term was confined to a particular sea. It does in fact actually occur in connection with the Gulf of Aqaba.

A point of departure for quite specific discussions has been provided by the exact-sounding indications of place in Ex. 14.2, which names the point where the Israelites camped shortly before the events at the sea. We are told that this lay 'in front of Pi-ha-hiroth, between Migdol and the sea, in front of Baal-zephon'. Baal-zephon is known as the shrine of a god Zeus Kasios, belonging to the Hellenistic-Roman period. It lies at the western end of a spit of land which divides Lake Sirbonis from the Mediterranean. Lake Sirbonis lies directly on the Mediterranean, on the coastline which leads over to Palestine from the eastern delta. The Israelites are said to have camped opposite Baal-zephon, which lies at the western end of the lake,[17] between Migdol and the sea. There is a Migdol in this region according to the statement of Egyptian sources as well,[18] in immediate proximity to the military road from Egypt to Palestine. Migdol even seems to have possessed an Egyptian military post of its own. The Israelites were apparently supposed to move north of this road, so that they penetrated into the region 'between Migdol and the sea', and in this way approached Baal-zephon at the sea, having it 'in front' of them, as the text says with its *lipne*. From there Lake Sirbonis spreads out towards the east and does actually block the direct coastal route to Palestine. One must avoid the lake region, though without being forced to cross the lake itself by boat. The question whether Lake Sirbonis could be the 'sea' at which the miraculous events of Ex. 14 and 15 took place has been given considerable impetus by Eissfeldt's investigations.[19] He pointed to a number of admittedly later but highly illuminating accounts by ancient writers, who talked about the nature of Lake Sirbonis. According to these, this lake at the edge of the Mediterranean had a character all its own. It was in various respects a highly dangerous 'lake'. Only a few examples can be quoted here. The following account comes from Diodorus Siculus *Bibliotheca historica*, 1.30:[20]

For between Coele Syria and Egypt there lies a lake, quite narrow but marvellously deep and some two hundred stades in length, which is called Serbonis and offers unexpected perils to those who approach it in ignorance of its nature. For since the body of the water is narrow, like a ribbon, and surrounded on all sides by great dunes, when there are constant south winds great quantities of sand are strewn over it. This sand hides the surface of the water and makes the outline of the lake contiguous with the solid land and entirely indistinguishable from it. For this reason many who were unacquainted with the peculiar nature of the place have disappeared together with whole armies, when they wandered from the beaten track. For as the sand is walked upon it gives way but gradually, deceiving with a kind of malevolent cunning those who advance upon it, until, suspecting some impending mishap, they begin to help one another only when it is no longer possible to turn back or escape. For anyone who has been sucked in by the mire cannot swim, since the slime prevents all movement of the body, nor is he able to wade out, since he has no solid footing; for by reason of the mixing of the sand with the water and the consequent change in the nature of both it comes about that the place cannot be crossed either on foot or by boat. Consequently those who enter upon these regions are borne towards the depths and have nothing to grasp to give them help, since the sand along the edge slips in with them. These flats have received a name appropriate to their nature as we have described it, being called Barathra [i.e. pits].

Some details of this description may seem curious, but what it means is clear enough. It must have been very shallow water, marshy at the edges especially, which can easily be misjudged and from which there is no escape once one has sunk deeply into it. But it is not only these natural conditions which make this region uncanny; in addition it is threatened by seaquakes. Strabo[21] gives an account of this, quite independently of Diodorus Siculus. He describes a war on the coast between Tyre and Ptolemais, and goes on:

At the time when the Ptolemaeans, after joining battle with Sarpedon the general, were left in this place, after a brilliant rout had taken place, a wave from the sea, like a flood-tide, submerged the fugitives; and some were carried off into the sea and destroyed, whereas others were left dead in the hollow places; and then, succeeding this wave, the ebb uncovered the shore again and disclosed the bodies of men lying promiscuously among dead fish. Like occurrences take place in the neighbourhood of the Mt Casius situated near Aegypt, where the land undergoes a single quick convulsion, and makes a sudden change to a higher or lower level, the result being that, whereas the elevated part repels the sea and the sunken part receives it, yet, the land makes a reverse change and the site resumes its old position again, a complete interchange of levels sometimes having taken place and sometimes not. Perhaps such disturbances are subject to periodic principles unknown to us, as is also said to be the case of the overflows of the Nile, which prove to be variant but follow some unknown order.

It is surely clear that 'the neighbourhood of the Mt Casius situated near Aegypt' mentioned here is another reminiscence of conditions at Lake Sirbonis. Moreover, though the account is not talking about biblical events, it describes them in a way which reminds us closely of the happenings in the Book of Exodus. The 'ebb' that follows the tidal wave allows land to appear again, with bodies lying about on it like dead fish. Exodus 14.30 brings a similar note to the effect that the bodies of the Egyptians lay on the sea shore, although actually the sea is supposed to have swallowed them up. Strabo expressly confirms in another passage[22] that the region of Lake Sirbonis was really subject to seaquakes in ancient times:

When I was residing in Alexandria, in Egypt, the sea about Pelusium and Mt Casius rose and flooded the country and made an island of the mountain, so that the road by Mt Casius into Phoenicia became navigable.

But this was the very road that the tribes coming from Egypt may once have taken!

It is tempting to see all these details in connection with what happened at the Reed Sea. For the departing groups, no doubt largely unfamiliar with the route, could well have entered the region of Lake Sirbonis; they could have strayed into conflict with Egyptian border groups stationed there or near there – troops which were destroyed, either because they did not know the character of the country, or because it was actually the very moment when a seaquake broke out. For the Israelites this astonishing disappearance of the enemy troops must have seemed like a miracle – and not unjustly. For at the decisive moment circumstances arose with which they could not possibly reckon, but which brought them complete deliverance. Not least, certain details in Ex. 14 become more explicable if one takes into account the conditions which have been described as existing at Lake Sirbonis. For the drying out of the sea through an east wind (the Yahwist's account) and the clogging of the chariot wheels (the Elohist version) would be quite understandable in this marshy ground, especially if a seaquake contributed to events, completing the 'divine visitation'. It was a short step to damming up the water into walls (the Priestly document), as the events were miraculously heightened. The idea of a 'crossing' of the sea can only have been derived from this Priestly version. For in reality Moses' people did not have to cross the sea along the line of the coast; they had at most to traverse its shores. This corresponds to the older accounts, which know nothing of a 'crossing', but which still give the sea as the reason for the extermination of the Egyptians. Conditions at Lake Sirbonis, as the ancient writers knew them, actually make an adequate step by step explanation of Ex. 14 possible. It ought, however, to be mentioned that the very exactness of the information and the possibilities of comparison made Noth sceptical about Eissfeldt's assertions.[23] He asks whether the precise local information in Ex. 14.2 (which belong to the latest stratum of the tradition, the Priestly document) could derive from the fact that people living later wanted to know more exactly where the Reed Sea miracle took place, since this was still unknown, and retrospectively localized it at Baal-zephon. This would mean that the local indications are secondary and that the actual place is still unknown, or could still be looked for elsewhere. This scepticism is, on a purely logical level, possible and the place where the Reed Sea miracle took place is certainly not provable with absolute certainty. But even if the local indications in Ex. 14.2 should be secondary, they still give a place which takes us with considerable accuracy right into the region where all the premises for the events at the sea were present. Even a secondary localization does not take place without any substantial reasons at all.[24]

In the framework of the biblical tradition, the shaping of the Reed Sea miracle would seem to be more important than the discussion about the place where it happened; for in the latest fragment, the great Song of Moses and the Israelites (Ex. 15.1–17), which has developed from the words of the ancient Song of Miriam, the event has been generously expanded, so that the happenings at the Reed Sea appear as the point of departure for the whole later history of Israel, right into the cultivated lands of Palestine. The development of the exodus tradition is here concentrated into a single document, which shows how Israel knew the way to go on thinking through ancient events and how, in a theological understanding of history, it interpreted and praised them as the acts of its God Yahweh.[25] This presents us with the basis for a final, concluding reflection. For what is found concentrated in Ex. 14 and 15 historically and as the history of a tradition, starting from the ancient unity of the Song of Miriam, through the different versions of events in ch. 14, down to the concept of ch. 15, expanded as it is into a theology of history – all this, which is found here in the narrowest space, is true in a wider sense of the whole exodus tradition and the happenings in Egypt which that tradition preserves.

VI

SURVEY: EVENT AND EFFECT

Noth called the familiar Old Testament phrase, 'Yahweh, who brought Israel out of Egypt', Israel's primal confession of faith.[1] In fact, the tradition about Egypt and Moses grew to play a dominant role in the Old Testament. It became Israel's classic tradition about the classical early period. In saying this we may leave the question uninvestigated as to whether this primal confession of faith was really equally well known and equally important in all parts of Israel from the very beginning.[2] Israel's complexity, especially in its early period, makes it understandable that these events, which were only experienced by a part of what later came to be Israel, could only gradually become a possession common to Israel as a whole.

I hope that in the course of this investigation and account the historical and theological presuppositions which made the period spent in Egypt by what were later Israelite tribes so important will have become clear. The events themselves can be fitted into a quite definite and limited space of time in the history of the ancient East, and the facts are confirmed by many details of the biblical tradition. What the semi-nomadic elements who penetrated into Egypt in the wake of the Aramaean migrations experienced there was an episode on the fringe of world history which found no record anywhere in the official documents of the great powers. Israel, however, recognized these experiences as one of the most important starting points of its existence as a people, a people which knew itself from that moment on to be borne up by the guidance of its God Yahweh. This combination of historical and theological insight, expressed in often individualistic composition, dominates the Book of Exodus, which is itself prepared for by the genealogical, family-history tradition of Genesis. The process of theological reflection has penetrated the Exodus account, in that basic reflections and recognitions were bound up with individual phases of events in Egypt and with the figure of Moses, and are positively anchored in the exodus event. Evidence of this are the pronouncements connected with the appearance of God to Moses, the attempts to interpret and to grasp the name of the deity and his nature once and for all. Historically and aetiologically the passover tradition is rooted in the exodus event, its customs being at the same time thereby historicized. Yahweh's powerful intervention in history, which secured the success of the exodus and thus Israel's further development, is documented by the broad tradition about the Reed Sea, which has its own nuances and independent growth. Step by step the path of the processing of tradition can be followed, from the starting point of its historical foundation – the path from the event to its effects, which extend in this case directly to the ethnic and religious self-understanding and self-consciousness of Israel.

Israel's sojourn in Egypt and the evidence that exists about it, whether this evidence comes from non-Israelite sources and illuminates these events indirectly, or whether, as in the Book of Exodus, it is bound up with the confession of faith in the God of Israel, reveals a fact that has often determined world history: it is not events themselves and their often insignificant radius of action that are capable of releasing far-reaching consequences; it is the depth of experience of the man who experiences those events. This depth of experience is set down in the biblical account and has never ceased to move the consciousness of Israel and the world to lasting reflection.

NOTES

INTRODUCTION

1. *Israel in Egypt*, text by Jennens, compiled from the Bible and the psalms of the Prayer Book, performed for the first time on 4 April 1739, in the King's Theatre, London.

2. The work was written between 1926 and 1942; to be precise, it was finished on 4 January 1943. *Joseph in Egypt* now appears as vol. 2, *Joseph the Provider* as vol. 3. The last volume was written in Mann's Californian exile. Morenz wonders whether Thomas Mann, who lived in Santa Monica, may perhaps have taken the expert advice of the Leipzig Egyptologist Georg Steindorff, who at that time was living close by (Morenz, 'Joseph in Ägypten', col. 401, n. 1). Von Rad, *Biblische Josephserzählung*, discusses Thomas Mann's work from the point of view of the Old Testament scholar.

3. Moses in the bulrushes, the burning bush and the passage through the sea have been especially popular themes from the period of the sojourn in Egypt. More rarely we see Moses negotiating with Pharaoh, or the labouring Israelites.

4. See the literature collected and cited in Rowley, *From Joseph*; Janssen, 'Publications'; Cazelles, 'Localisations'; also the references in Fohrer, *Exodus*, and Schmid, *Mose*.

5. For the manifold influences of Egypt on the west see now Morenz, *Begegnung*, and further the same author's illuminating and stimulating study on the Magic Flute. For Egyptian influence abroad in ancient times see Morenz, *Ägyptische Religion*, pp. 244–73.

I

1. Gen. 11.28–12.3. The home of Abraham and his kinsmen, or at least the decisive starting points for the migration to Palestine, lie in the Haran area of Upper Mesopotamia. Whether the Ur of the Chaldaeans of Gen. 11.28 means the Ur that was situated in the heart of Sumeria, in southern Mesopotamia, still remains problematical. The fact that scholars such as de Vaux and others answer this question in the affirmative (and therefore also reckon with Abraham's migration from Ur to Haran) is connected essentially with their dating of Abraham to the first half of the second millennium BC and with an extensive development of the patriarchal families, which goes together with

this date. I have maintained a different view below. Cf. de Vaux, RB 55, pp.321ff.; also RB 72, pp.10ff. On the history of research since Wellhausen, with extensive bibliographical references, cf. Weidmann, *Patriarchen*. Parrot, *Abraham*, gives a general introduction, which also covers the archaeological problems, with maps and illustrations.

2. It is different with the transmission of the laws in the Pentateuch; these are for the most part assigned to the stratum of tradition known as the Priestly document and take account of Israel's division into twelve tribes. For an explanation of the facts see the present writer's recent article 'Autonome Entwicklungen', pp.156f.

3. Details and evidence in Herrmann, *Heilserwartungen*, pp.64ff.

II

1. Albright, 'Abram the Hebrew ; de Vaux, *Patriarchen* and *Patriarchenerzählungen*. See also ch. I, n. 1 above.

2. Cornelius' miscellany, 'Mose urkundlich', rests on uncritical combinations of different sources. According to the report of Manetho, passed down to us in Josephus, *Contra Apionem* I, 26, there was a 'rebellion by Moses', more precisely a rebellion on the part of the priest Osarsiph of Heliopolis. This Moses ruled over Egypt for thirteen years. There actually was a usurper Amenmose, who probably lies behind a once-mentioned *Mŝyy* (Pap. Salt 124, verso II, 17/18; cf. J. Černý, JEA 15, 1929, p.146 and pl. 44) and who must be fitted in either between Merneptah and Sethos II (W. Helck, ZDMG 105, 1955, pp.39ff.) or as counter-claimant to Sethos II (J. von Beckerath, ZDMG 106, 1956, pp.246ff.). Cornelius wants to make a distinction between the 'Moses' mentioned by Manetho and the usurper Amenmose, but would obviously like to identify one of them with the Moses of the Bible, who, as an official in the last years of Merneptah's reign, is to be brought into accord with the biblical evidence. All this is hypothesis, not to say fantasy. None of the attempted identifications can be proved, quite apart from other counter-arguments.

3. Literally 'the walls of the ruler'.

4. The story rests on sound historical knowledge and purports to be an inscription in Sinuhe's tomb. It is written in the first person. Transmitted on two papyri dating from the end of the Middle Kingdom; parts of the text on numerous ostraca. For a translation see Pritchard, ANET, pp.18–22, from whom this rendering is taken.

5. Berlin manuscript B 15–28.

6. See Posener's view of the Sinuhe story in *Littérature*, pp.87ff.

7. Separate consideration of this section by Scharff, *Der historische Abschnitt*. The translation here is taken from Pritchard, ANET, p.416.

8. *Merikare* ll. 91–100.

9. Circumlocution for the beginning of early times, when the king-god Horus himself ruled. The meaning is that the Bedouin customs have been known from time immemorial.

10. These words are an expression of the Egyptian king's determination.

We are reminded of the 'I am who I am' of Ex. 3.14. The comparable nature of the two passages is considered in ch. V below.

11. *Prophecy of Neferti* (earlier usual transliteration: Nefer-rehu), ll.66–68. Translation in Pritchard, ANET, pp. 444–6.

12. Posener, 'Asiatiques'; the writer concerns himself especially with the important papyrus Brooklyn 35, 1446, which was published by W. C. Hayes. See also Helck, *Beziehungen*, pp. 79ff. In this connection, attention must also be drawn to the famous picture from Khnum-hotep's tomb in Beni Hasan, dating from the period *c.* 1890 BC. It shows a caravan of 17 people, who are apparently coming from the Syrian region and crave entry into Egypt (Pritchard, ANEP, pl. 3). Scholars generally use the word 'slaves' in connection with these elements of the population, saying that it was as slaves that they lived in Egypt. But if by slaves one understands people who count as chattels and are accordingly only subject to the law of property – i.e., that which can be disposed of at will by sale, exchange, hire or gift – the term is, with a few exceptions, inapposite, down to the New Kingdom. It was only the great number of prisoners of war who appeared on the Egyptian scene at this later period who were for the first time subjected to a slave existence without rights, of the kind indicated here. Up to then it is more appropriate not to talk unhesitatingly about slaves, but rather about different grades of service which the non-Egyptian elements of the population carried out in Egyptian society. On the differentiation in the social categories see also Posener, op. cit., p. 147. For the rejection of the ideologically loaded term 'slave-owning state' see Morenz, *Ägypten und das Berliner Ägyptische Museum*, pp. 33f.

13. The relevant section of Manetho's history has been preserved, together with some secondary additions, by the Jewish writer Josephus in *Contra Apionem* I 14 §§75ff. (*c.* AD 100).

14. Meyer, *Geschichte des Altertums*, I 2, pp. 312ff, also talked about the 'kingdom of the Hyksos'.

15. A view recently supported by Helck, *Beziehungen*, pp. 92ff. It is justly subjected to critical examination by von Beckerath, *Zweite Zwischenzeit*, pp. 113ff.

16. Alt, *Herkunft der Hyksos*, pp 72ff. Alt's views are endorsed by Posener, 'Asiatiques', pp. 161ff., and are frequently adopted with approval elsewhere, e.g. by Vercoutter in *Die Altorientalischen Reiche*, I, pp. 350ff.

17. The widely scattered literature on the Hyksos question has not yet been systematically collected. The relevant works already cited here mention numerous monographs. See also the bibliography in van Seters, *Hyksos*, though his own investigation of the Hyksos question is problematical.

18. See James, *Egypt*, and the literature he cites.

19. 'Amorites' means 'people of the west', 'people from Amurru'. The expression is still in favour even today, though to a limited degree. Cf. de Vaux, RB 53, pp. 338f.; id., RB 72, pp. 13ff.; Kupper, *Nomades*, pp. 147ff.; id, *Northern Mesopotamia*.

20. Bauer, *Ostkanaanäer* (a philological and historical investigation of the nomadic section of the 'Amorites' in Babylon).

21. The expression dates back to Hommel, *Altisraelitische Überlieferung*.

22. For example by Noth, *Ursprünge*, p. 29; he suggested the term as long

ago as 1928 in his book on Israelite personal names, then abandoned it for a time (ZDPV 65, 1942, p. 34, n. 2), but later adopted it once more in connection with the Mari texts.

23. The parallels between certain legal precepts in Hammurabi's so-called Codex and certain laws in the Old Testament are due to their mediation through Canaanite law, in as far as we can trace the process in detail at all. It is only in a very wide and indirect sense that legal usages common to the Mesopotamian collections of laws can be drawn on in support of direct ethnic, historical and sociological connections. To interpret narrative details in the patriarchal tradition with reference to legal history (recently above all by comparison with family-law regulations in the Nuzi texts) is no doubt instructive; but it offers no sound criteria for assessing the temporal or geographical setting of the patriarchs. De Vaux deals with the relevant problems, giving some examples, in RB 72, pp. 21ff.

24. Soden, *Aufstieg des Assyrerreiches*.

25. Otten, in *Die Altorientalischen Reiche*, II, pp. 128ff.; see also Hauschild, *Arier*.

26. For the history, and especially the chronology, of the New Kingdom, see Hornung, *Untersuchungen*.

27. There are numerous detailed investigations of the Pharaohs' city lists in essay and monograph form, and these are constantly being supplemented and enriched by new contributions. For a summary, see especially Simons, *Handbook*, and Noth, 'Wege der Pharaonenheere'. See also the lists of the places mentioned in Pritchard, ANET, pp. 242f.

28. The faith encouraged by Amenophis IV was directed mainly towards worship of the solar disc (*itn*, generally rendered as Aten) but it is not entirely free from the structure of Egyptian theology. The full dogmatic name for the sun god of Amarna was: 'Re-Harachte, who rejoices in the horizon, in his name as Shu, which is Yati (= Aten).' Morenz (*Ägyptische Religion*, pp. 154ff.) has made it seem probable that in this formula the old sun god of Helioplis, Re, is equated with the new manifestation Aten (= Yati) and with Shu. Shu is originally the god of the air, later also a younger form of the sun god (Bonnet, *Reallexikon*, pp. 686ff.). The king-god was able to equate himself with Shu as the son of Re. In this equation Re = Shu = Aten, the sun, i.e., the king, is as it were raised to the highest divine plane and, together with Re and Aten, forms an almost trinitarian unity, in which at the same time a father-son relationship between the deities continues to operate, finding its completion in Aten. What is often claimed to be Amarna 'monotheism', which allegedly manifested itself in the general belief in the solar disc (which is what is meant by Aten), is an assertion derived from the premises of Western thinking. In reality, several deities are absorbed into an all-embracing divine figure, as happened fairly frequently in the course of Egyptian religious history. One can at most talk about monotheistic tendencies in Egyptian religion, but not about monotheism, in the sense of the exclusive worship of a single deity.

29. The Egyptian name for the capital was *ȝḫ.t-'Itn*, 'The horizon of Aten'.

30. In Egyptian *ȝḫ-n-'Itn*, whereby the king demonstrates in a particular way his worship of 'Aten' and his closeness to him.

31. This also applies particularly to the strongly individualistic art of the Amarna period. See Schäfer, *Amarna*. Cf. also accounts of Egyptian history and art as a whole.

32. What are known as the Amarna Letters give a vivid picture of this. The letters are the official correspondence of the kings of Mitanni, Assur and Babylon (as well as the more minor rulers of Syria and Palestine) with Amenophis III and IV. Most of them are written in Akkadian. Typical of the letters are the complaints of these foreign princes about the lack of activity and support from the side of the Egyptian king. The letters are informative about conditions in Palestine. They are translated in Pritchard, ANET, pp. 483–90.

33. Carter-Mace, *The Tomb of Tut-Ankh-Amen*.

34. On the chronological problems see Hornung, *Untersuchungen*.

35. Alt, *Deltaresidenz*, pp. 176–85.

36. See ch. IV below.

37. Helck, *Beziehungen*, pp. 208ff., gives a detailed account of the events (with tactical diagrams), taking recent research into account.

38. At the mouth of the *nahr el-kelb*, a little north of Beirut, a prominent ridge of rock thrusts forward almost to the coast. Among the numerous reliefs and inscriptions, both ancient and modern, which are to be found there, is a relief of Ramesses II (though today it is only in a poor state of preservation).

39. The original text, engraved in cuneiform script on a silver tablet, has been lost. Two Egyptian copies exist, on stelae in the temples of Karnak and Ramesseum, as well as a clay tablet copy from Ḫattuša-Boghazköi, the capital of the Hittite kingdom. There is a comparison of the two texts by Langdon and Gardiner, *Treaty*, pp. 179ff.; see also Pritchard, ANET, pp. 199ff.

40. Cf. Noth, *Ursprünge*; Ebeling-Meissner, 'Aramu' in *Reallexikon* I, pp. 131ff.; Scharff-Moortgat, *Ägypten und Vorderasien*, pp. 379ff.; Dupont-Sommer, *Araméens* and 'Débuts de l'histoire araméenne'; Moscati, *Geschichte und Kultur* (German trans. of *Storia e civiltà dei Semiti*), pp. 148ff.; id., 'Ahlamu'; Weippert, *Settlement*, pp. 102ff., especially p. 103, n. 5.

III

1. De Vaux, RB 72, pp. 15ff. In general Moscati, *Semites*; Kupper, *Nomades*.

2. We may think of the state of Bît Adîni on the Upper Euphrates, with its centre Til Barsip, or the state of Bît Bachjâni in the Chabur valley, with its centre in Guzana (Tell Halaf). Later the state of Sam'al developed in Cilicia and the state of Bît Agushi in Northern Syria, round Arpad and Aleppo.

3. Attempts to identify this Aramaean who is described as 'my father' with any one of the patriarchs known to us is probably a mistake. 'Father' is here the prototype of the ancestor from whom, according to the principle of genealogical thinking, a people is derived.

4. This can also be deduced from the sequence of place names in Gen. 10.19; after the mention of Gerar and Gaza, the border line indicated turns consistently inland, touching Sodom and some other settlements, which must be put east of it.

5. Albright, 'Abram the Hebrew', discusses and partly accepts the earlier views expounded by Gordon and Nougayrol. A short summary with references may be found in de Vaux, RB 72, pp. 18ff.

6. The Hebrew word *sāḥar*, attested by Gen. 23.16; 34.10:42.34, is appealed to in proof. In Speiser's view (BASOR 164, 1961, pp. 23ff.) this means 'to trade', but in classical Hebrew it means 'to wander about', which fits in far better with the way of life and living conditions of the patriarchs. See also de Vaux, op. cit. p. 22.

7. De Vaux claims for the patriarchs the considerable space of time between 1900 and 1700 BC and would like to fit the migration of Jacob's sons to Egypt into the framework of the Hyksos movement. He even sees this as being 'the least uncertain combination' of the documents at our disposal (RB 55, p. 336), and finds 'no better framework' in the second millennium before Christ into which the patriarchal stories could be fitted (*Patriarchenerzählungen*, p. 36). Bright (pp. 81ff.) pleads for the same period and believes that the patriarchs were 'heads of large clans' (p. 75).

8. Abraham's migration to Egypt (Gen. 12.10–20) is problematical, historically speaking; the narrative motif of 'danger to the mother of the race' which is employed here recurs in Gen. 20 and 26.1ff., but there, significantly, not in the context of Egypt and the Pharaoh but in connection with Abimelech, king of Gerar. Moreover, in Gen. 26 the motif is transferred to Isaac. The form-critical problems are discussed in exemplary fashion by Koch in *Growth*, pp. 111–32. Bright considers that Joseph's move to Egypt took place in the Hyksos period (p. 85).

9. The theory once more finds support recently in Cazelles, 'Moses', p. 17; he has Moses educated at the fourteenth-century Egyptian court. Rowley, *From Joseph*, pp. 116ff., transplants Joseph into the Akhenaten period.

10. For a discussion about the nature of the Amarna religion, see ch. II above. The catchword 'monotheistic' has obscured more than it has clarified in this context, and has wrongly permitted highly differing developments to appear comparable.

11. The term 'proto-Israelite' for the elements of the later Israel which had been in Egypt is sometimes used to distinguish them from the 'proto-Aramaean' ancestors of Israel from Mesopotamia; but it has the disadvantage of being open to misunderstanding if one is not aware of the terminological convention, especially since the name Israel in particular had nothing to do originally with the groups which came from Egypt. Koch argues differently in 'Tod des Religionsstifters', p. 107, n. 27.

12. De Vaux, *Patriarchen*, pp. 3ff., and *Patriarchenerzählungen*, pp. 11ff. Noth devoted equivalent attention to the formation of proper names but comes to more discriminating historical conclusions. See in particular Noth, 'Mari und Israel', and *Ursprünge*, pp. 12ff. For a basic study see Noth, *Personennamen*.

13. For the definition of this term see ch. II above.

14. The typical features of these names, especially the names of the patriarchs, are covered by Noth in his study 'Mari und Israel'. For Abraham or Abram in particular, see pp. 143ff., and *Personennamen*, p. 52.

15. Noth rests his theory of the 'proto-Aramaean' character of this

linguistic stratum very largely on these so-called 'imperfect forms', *Personen-namen*, pp. 43ff.

16. Noth, *Personennamen*, pp. 52ff.

17. The stock of names here shows greater irregularity of type, where we can distinguish at all with certainty between earlier and later names. Names like Amram and Abihu seem to be more comprehensible structurally than, for example, Aaron, Nadab, Jochebed, Gersom and Miriam.

18. See also Herrmann, 'Der alttestamentliche Gottesname'.

19. Yahweh as a theophorous element is only dominant in Israelite names from the beginning of the monarchy onward. Only five names are known to us from the period of the judges which can be held to contain the name Yahweh: Joash (Judg. 6.11 and frequently elsewhere); Jotham (Judg. 9.5ff.); Micah or Micaiah (Judg. 17.1; 4.5ff.); Jonathan (Judg. 18.30); Joel (I Sam. 8.2). From the pre-judges period only Joshua comes into question. Noth, *Personennamen*, pp. 107 and 112ff.

20. Noth rejects the suggestion (*Personennamen*, pp. 108ff.). For a discussion of the facts see Driver, 'Original Form', and the more recent investigations by Murtonen, *Divine Names*, and Maclaurin, 'YHWH'.

21. On the Shasu see Helck, *Beziehungen*, passim (see index), especially pp. 278ff. Typical characteristics were already discussed by Müller in *Asien und Europa*, p. 135. Helck, 'Bedrohung', pp. 477ff., draws attention to an interesting fact which he calls an Egyptian 'linguistic rule'. In reference to the movements of population south of a line from Raphia to the southern end of the Dead Sea and its eastern shore, the Egyptians, from the middle of the eighteenth dynasty right down to the times of Ramesses II, talked about *ꜣꜣśw*, whereas they cover the movements north of this line by the term *'prw*, which we shall have to discuss further, but which is probably identical with *ḫabiru*. Helck would like to see the same immigrant movement from the east behind both terms. This is deserving of attention, as a basic observation. The different terminology may be connected with the fact that the Egyptians in the northern area were accustomed to talk about *'prw*, while in the south they spoke of *ꜣꜣśw*. Helck admits that this terminology was probably retained while the phenomena themselves changed in the course of time. At the beginning it may have been only scattered groups to whom the Egyptians gave the name, but it can later have been complete tribes. It will be permissible to draw the conclusion from these statements of Helck's that the Egyptian sources (though admittedly without discriminating closely) cover in a suitable way movements of population which will have been directly connected with the increasing activity of the Aramaeans.

22. The problems involved are discussed by Herrmann in 'Der alttestamentliche Gottesname', where the Egyptian evidence is cited, especially that produced by Leclant from Soleb. A synopsis of the argument may also be found in the *Papers I* of the Fourth World Congress of Jewish Studies, pp. 213–6. See also now Helck, 'Bedrohung', pp. 477f.

23. Pap. Anastasi VI, 51–61. Text: Gardiner, *Late-Egyptian Miscellanies*, pp. 76f.; translation with commentary: Caminos, *Late-Egypt. Misc.*, pp. 293ff.; see also Pritchard, ANET, p. 259, followed here with minor adjustments. For the 'frontier post register' of a frontier official at the time of Merneptah

(*c.* 1221 BC), which sheds light on the routine frontier traffic experienced by Egyptian officials, see Galling, *Textbuch*, pp. 37f.

24. 'Edom' is the usual translation here, although nothing definite can be said about the locality presupposed. Edom probably also occurs in the list of Pharaoh Shoshenk. See Noth, ZDPV 61, 1938, p. 295.

25. The successor of Ramesses II (*c.* 1223–1203); but Merneptah's successor Sethos II (*c.* 1203–1194) also had Merneptah as the second part of his name. Edel, *Textbuch*, p. 40, n. 3, talks about the possibility that the fortress was called after the latter.

26. Latterly Helck would like to identify this place Ṯkw with the Pithom mentioned in Ex. 1.11 and to localize it on the *tell el-mashūta* in the eastern delta. See his 'Ṯkw und die Ramsesstadt', VT 15, 1965, pp. 35–40.

27. I.e., the eighth year of the reign of Sethos II.

28. These are the five days which were added to the twelve months of thirty days in order to bring the calendar into line with the solar year.

29. This is the third of the intercalary days (see preceding note).

30. Refers to the official note of arrivals, probably their numerical strength. Similarly in the caption accompanying the picture of the caravan from the Beni Hasan tomb (Pritchard, ANEP, pl. 3): 'List of Bedouins . . . In all 37 desert Bedouins.'

31. The Edomites mainly inhabited the mountains on the east side of *wādi el-'araba*, the narrow valley which adjoins the southern end of the Dead Sea. In the Old Testament this central Edomite area is almost always identical with the mountains of Se'ir. Noth, *The Old Testament World*, pp. 57 and 79. But on the 'Shasu tribes of Edom' see n. 24 above.

32. *Neferti* 66–68: Pritchard, ANET, p. 446. See also ch. II above.

33. Helck's view, op. cit. He assumes that 'Pithom' – as can hardly be doubted – can be explained as deriving from a *pr-Itm* 'temple of Atum'. This temple would have existed near the fort in the centre of the city and would have given its name to the city of Ṯkw, according to the custom (known from the time of the Ramesses) of no longer calling places by their old names but of giving them the name of their chief temple. According to an earlier, admittedly disputed, view, Pithom was to be sought near the *tell er-reṭābe*. Gardiner, JEA 5, 1918, pp. 267ff.; for another view, E. Naville, JEA 10, 1924, pp. 32ff.; for Gardiner's answer, ibid., pp. 95f. See also Peet, *Egypt and the Old Testament*, pp. 86ff., and Gardiner, JEA 19, 1933, p. 127.

34. Bardtke, *Vom Nildelta zum Sinai*, conveys a graphic impression of this area.

35. Gen. 45.10; 47.4, 6 and frequently elsewhere; see also Ex. 8.18; 9.26.

36. See primarily the brief survey in Alt, *Deltaresidenz*, which also has a bibliography.

37. On both questions see now Helck, 'Ṯkw', in controversy with Redford, VT 13, pp. 401ff.

38. The French excavations were led by P. Montet. A summarized account may be found in Montet, *Tanis*.

39. Mahmud Hamza was responsible for the diggings; he was commissioned by the Egyptian Department of Antiquities. Cf. his report in *Annales du Service des Antiquités de l'Égypte* (ASAE) 30, 1930, pp. 31ff.

40. Alt, *Deltaresidenz*. Amenophis IV's capital extended about nine miles from north to south and about twelve miles from west to east, according to the evidence of the surviving frontier steles.

41. Gen. 46.31–34 witnesses to the pride of the free Bedouins, who for generations lived as herdsmen. Helck's view (already expressed in *Beziehungen*, p. 613, and repeated in his article 'Die Bedrohung Palästinas', p. 480, n. 1) is that the Semitic groups who were employed in the building at Pithom and Ramesses did not belong to nomadic tribes who had infiltrated into Egypt, but were prisoners of war such as can be seen in the picture on the wall of Rekh-mi-Re's tomb (ANEP, pl. 35; the period of Thutmosis III). This must be disputed, however, for several reasons. Prisoners of war in every period are usually anxious to return home after their escape and not to begin a quite different form of existence, as Helck thinks was the case in the prisoners-of-war section at Pithom and Ramesses. They are supposed to have 'joined up with nomadic tribes'. Or are we to assume that they were *ꜣꜣšw* who had been conscripted somewhere? This is inevitably to enter the field of speculation. If one went along with Helck's thesis, it would mean that the exodus tradition, which became so important for Israel's history, went back ultimately to a group of people who originally had nothing to do with later Israel at all, but whose experiences became a firm part of the reminiscences of the nomadic tribe 'which they joined'. To this it must quite simply be said: the rise of the Old Testament traditions, their content, and the whole history of their influence all combine to contradict the view that they began with a 'prisoner of war experience'. It is probably more plausible to trace back the kernel of the Egyptian experiences to tribal traditions, which lived on in unbroken narrative practice and were evoked by events which this particular tribe itself experienced – not to happenings which it took over from a group completely strange to it, and which was probably complex in origin. It is worth pointing out that the view expounded by Helck in his *Beziehungen* (p. 613) is not found in this form in Noth's *Geschichte Israels* (sic!), pp. 97ff.

42. On this see also the extensive discussion by Cazelles, 'Localisations'. Redford maintains the view (which would seem to be untenable) that Ex. 1. 11b, with its specific localizations, Pithom and Ramesses, goes back to a gloss interpolated by P and cannot have been made in its present form before the end of the seventh century BC. The intention was a subsequent exact localization of Israel's stay. Now, the place name Ramesses disappears in later Egyptian tradition, being replaced, according to a probably correct view, by the name Tanis. That the name of the city of Ramesses should nevertheless penetrate into the Israelite tradition at a later point, when it no longer played any part among the Egyptians, is thought even by Alt to be improbable (*Deltaresidenz*, p. 184, n. 4), especially in view of the material collected by Gardiner from the period of the nineteenth and twentieth dynasties (JEA 5, 1918, pp. 127ff., 179ff., 242ff.). See also Gardiner, *Onomastica* II, pp. 171ff. (No. 410).

43. The tradition of the 'assembly of Shechem' in Josh. 24 no doubt presupposes the final result of this process; there the acceptance of the Yahweh religion is concentrated in a single confessional act, made on Joshua's initiative.

44. This list material in Genesis, and especially its crystallization into a

rounded, systematic fixed form, must in all probability be assigned to the period when the traditions of the early period were classified and collected for the first time in Israel; that is to say, the early monarchy. It may be largely true that behind it there was also the intention of providing a political justification for the formation of the Davidic empire, on the basis of a systematic genealogy. On this point see the further discussion about the place of the twelve-tribe idea in the history of the Old Testament tradition in Herrmann, 'Autonome Entwicklungen', pp. 150ff.

45. In his books on Israel's twelve-tribe system and on the history of Israel, Noth made it seem emphatically probable that we have here to do with 'amphictonies' on the Greek and early Italian pattern; but this has recently become questionable. It at least demands a differentiation appropriate to early Israel. See Fohrer's general survey, '"Amphiktyonie" und "Bund"?'

46. That according to Ex. 6.2ff. Moses had this revelation directly in the land of Egypt, and that he was called there, is a favourite thesis. It has no basis in the text itself. It is part of the character of this Priestly section, which is conceived without local reminiscence, that it sets no store by the place where the event takes place, but attaches importance solely to the exposition of the theological statement that El Shaddai is identical with Yahweh. Exodus 6 therefore offers no historically relevant counter-evidence to the supposition that the original place of the revelation was in the desert.

47. See the details already given above and Herrmann, 'Der alttestamentliche Gottesname'.

48. Posener, 'Asiatiques'; Janssen, 'Fonctionnaires'; Helck, *Beziehungen*, pp. 79ff., 359ff.

49. Pritchard, ANET, p. 260.

50. Vergote, *Joseph en Égypte*; there is a detailed discussion of the book by Morenz, *Joseph in Ägypten*. Since then many critical voices have been raised against Vergote's basic conception. See among others Herrmann, *Joseph in Ägypten*. On the Egyptological background of the Joseph story see also Janssen, 'Egyptological Remarks'.

51. In favour of this is also the prominent treatment of Joseph and his territory in the ancient tribal sayings in Gen. 49.22–26; Deut. 33.13–17. On this see in detail Zobel, *Stammesspruch und Geschichte*, pp. 112ff. The historical problems are dealt with in Kaiser, 'Stammesgeschichtliche Hintergründe'.

52. Joseph was born of Rachel, who was at first barren (Gen. 30.22–25); and when Benjamin is born, Rachel dies (Gen. 35.16–20).

53. Kaiser, op. cit.; Schunck, *Benjamin*; Täubler, *Biblische Studien*, pp. 176ff.

54. Von Rad, 'The Joseph Narrative and Ancient Wisdom'.

55. See details in the works mentioned in n. 50 above.

56. This was due in no small part to the fact that 'Hebrew' became the name for the main language of the Old Testament, and that the users of this idiom were therefore called 'Hebrews'. 'Hebrew' as the name for a language is first to be met with in rabbinic literature. There is no evidence for it in the Old Testament, but it is no doubt fairly early in date. Meyer, *Hebräische Grammatik* II, p. 11.

57. Survey of the distribution of the word in the Old Testament in Koch, 'Hebräer', pp. 40ff.

58. Gen. 14.13.; Ex. 21.2.

59. In the Masoretic text there are eighteen passages. The word is used in Ex. 1.22 only in the Samaritan text and in the Septuagint. For details see Koch, op. cit.

60. The evidence is collected in Bottéro, *Problème des Ḫabiru*, and in Greenberg, *Ḫab/piru*. For further bibliography see Koch, op. cit., p.38, n. 2. See also the detailed section 'Apiru and Hebrews' in Weippert, *Settlement*, pp.63–102.

61. Details in de Vaux, RB 72, pp. 19ff.; see especially p.20, n. 64.

62. Koch gives a brief summing up of the state of research, op. cit., pp. 37ff.

63. See Posener in Bottéro, *Problème des Ḫabiru*, pp. 166f.

64. Posener in Bottéro, op. cit., pp. 173ff.

65. The material presented by Posener in Bottéro (op. cit., pp. 165ff.) may be found in Edel's German translation in Galling, *Textbuch*, pp. 34ff.

66. Koch, 'Hebräer', pp. 71ff.

67. The 'small-scale' theory is supported here not so much with an eye to local conditions; the main point is the possibility of surveying the people involved in these actions, who for their part remain conceivable as the bearers of mutually complementary historical traditions.

IV

1. See Möhlenbrink, 'Die levitischen Überlieferungen'; Gunneweg, *Leviten und Priester*; Noth, *Überlieferungsgeschichte*, pp. 195ff.; Schmid, *Mose*, pp. 36ff., 85ff.

2. Smend, *Mosebild*, gives a detailed account, with the evidence.

3. Smend's account (see previous note) is mainly systematic. Osswald, *Bild des Mose*, gives in contrast a chronological account of Moses research since Wellhausen. See Schmid, *Mose*, for the latest state of research. See also especially Cazelles' article 'Pentateuque', which incorporates a wealth of material.

4. Noth, *Überlieferungsgeschichte*.

5. Up to now no separate monograph has been devoted exclusively to the contesting of Noth's view; as a rule it has been treated only in connection with other themes. Von Rad, *Theology*, I, pp. 289ff., confines himself to a description of the changes in views about Moses and his office in the framework of the Pentateuchal sources. The dissertations by Seebass and Schnutenhaus are concerned with questions of detail, as is Seebass, *Erzvater Israel*, pp. 56ff. Moses' connection with Sinai has attracted special attention: Smend, *Jahwekrieg und Stämmebund*, pp. 87ff.; Gese, 'Bemerkungen zur Sinaitradition'. For the Sinai tradition in particular see Beyerlin. Origins and History, and Eissfeldt, *Komposition der Sinai-Erzählung*. On the general principles of research on the Pentateuch, see Herrmann, 'Mose', pp. 318ff.

6. The name type R^ζ-*mś* = Ramose '(the God) Re is born' must be distinguished from R^ζ-*mś*(y)-*św* = Ramesses '(the God) Re has given birth to him'. In the first case we have a form of the so-called pseudo-participle, and in the second the active perfect participle, really, 'It is Re who has given birth to him'. This interpretation is also confirmed by the cuneiform *Ria-maśśi*, 'Ramose',

as over against *Ri-a-ma-še-ša*, 'Ramesses'. See Edel, 'Neue keilschriftliche Umschreibungen', pp. 17, 22. I hope that this will serve to clear up the statements in my article 'Mose' (p. 33), which are open to misunderstanding at this point. On the much discussed problem of the transformation of the *s* sound, *š* in *mśy*, in contrast to *š* in Hebrew *moše*, see Griffiths, 'Egyptian Derivation'; Helck, 'Ṯkw', pp. 43ff.

7. For details see Griffiths, op. cit. The explanation of the name in Ex. 2.10 via the Hebrew verb *mšh* is 'popular etymology'.

8. This too can be called in question in view of the fact that Egyptian names do occasionally turn up in Israel otherwise. In the case of Moses, however, the detailed circumstances of his activity may also be allowed some weight. That the man who had become of such decisive importance for Israel's religion should not have an Israelite name is a fact which could hardly be derived from secondary circumstances.

9. It was already possible in Egyptian for the name to be limited to its second element. See Griffiths, op. cit., pp. 226ff.

10. Hayes, *Papyrus*, pp. 87ff. and plates 8–13; discussed by Posener in 'Asiatiques'; see also Herrmann, 'Mose', pp. 305ff.

11. Hayes, op. cit., verso p. 35; the first element of the Semitic name is 'Baal', without the 'l', which is alien to Egyptian.

12. Verso l. 36.

13. Posener, op. cit., passim; Janssen, 'Fonctionnaires'; Helck, *Beziehungen*, pp. 79ff., 359ff.

14. Gen. 39.7–18.

15. Ex. 2.1–10.

16. The term 'adoption' is a possible one for this proceeding, but it should not be forced into a strict legal meaning. We have examples of legal acts of this kind dating from the late New Kingdom. See Helck–Otto, *Kleines Wörterbuch*, p. 27. On the question of adoption in the Old Testament against the background of cuneiform law, see now Donner, 'Adoption oder Legitimation?'

17. This story quite certainly uses common motifs from sagas and legends in which the theme is the endangering and deliverance soon after birth of what were later to be important people. Material of this kind is mentioned and discussed by Jeremias, *Das Alte Testament*, pp. 400ff., and by Gressmann, *Mose*, 7ff. This should not, of course, lead us to overlook the fact that each of these stories shares certain characteristics of the cultural sphere from which it derives and about which it tells.

18. Ex. 2.11ff.

19. Ex. 3.

20. See ch. II above.

21. Noth, *Exodus*, p. 32.

22. Ex. 3.18; 5.1–3; 7.16, 26; 8.16; 9.1, 13.

23. As Gunneweg does in 'Mose in Midian'.

24. Galling, *Textbuch*, p. 40f. See ch. III above on this point.

25. Though it is true that the passages in question belong to later tradition: Num. 14.34 (P); Deut. 2.7; 8.2ff.; 29.5. In the case of the two passages in Amos (Amos 2.10 and 5.25) assignment to the eighth century prophet is doubtful because of the context.

26. The conclusion is sometimes drawn from this that in this passage the Septuagint is limiting the period in Egypt to merely 215 years. Thus Josephus (*Antt.* II, 15.2) already related the 430 years to the period between Abraham and the exodus, which elicits the highly schematic halving of the number 430. See Montet, *Das alte Ägypten*, pp. 20f.

27. For a fundamental study see Noth, *Überlieferungsgeschichtliche Studien.*

28. Noth, op. cit., pp. 18ff.

29. De Vaux (in RB 72, p. 27) also sees the difficulties involved in the acceptance of a stay in Egypt lasting 400 years, but he thinks a solution is possible. See also de Vaux, RB 55, pp. 336f.

30. See here Alt, 'The Settlement of the Israelites', pp. 133ff. The mention of the name Israel on the Merneptah stele, which is usually included in these discussions, still has no established relationship to the statements of the Old Testament. Complete text of the stele in Gressmann, AOT, pp. 20ff.; see also Pritchard, ANET p. 378, and Galling, *Textbuch*, pp. 39ff. (with a more up to date bibliography). The age of the relevant section remains disputed. Helck ('Bedrohung', p. 479) thinks it possible, in view of the places other than Israel mentioned on the Merneptah stele, that events are reflected which already took place under Ramesses II, or even earlier, under Sethos I. But it should be clear that, from the perspective of the Old Testament and in view of the wide differences in the occupation of land by Israelite tribes, we are not forced absolutely to assign this section of the Israel stele to the period of Ramesses II or Merneptah. Since the name Israel was already associated with Jacob (Gen. 32), it is not out of the question to identify the 'Israel' group meant on the stele with a section of the tribes of what later became Israel, which had already found a foothold before the arrival of the 'house of Joseph'. Noth once thought particularly of the tribes who were said to be descended from Leah (Noth, *System*, p. 92); later he took a more sceptical view (*Überlieferungsgeschichte*, p. 278, n. 655; *History of Israel*, p. 3). That an Egyptian source should be familiar with 'Israel' as a power at all is important enough; but this single piece of evidence does not allow us to draw definite inferences about a particular phase of Israel's early history.

V

1. The narrative structure of the chapter in question, Ex. 3, is easily grasped. The relatively self-contained scene of the burning bush (vv. 1–5), which is designed to prove the sacred character of the place, is followed (vv. 6–12) by God's first speech, which already contains the deity's presentation of himself, the announcement of the liberation from Egypt and the promise of the cultivated land of Canaan. Moses is given the task of negotiating with the Pharaoh and of preparing the exodus of the Israelites. Verses 13 and 14 bring Moses' question about the divine name, and the subsequent response, which is continued in v. 15 after a new introduction; in vv. 16–22 this passes directly into a further divine speech, in which Moses is told to hand on his commission to the elders of the Israelites. The dialogue between God and Moses finds its continuation in Ex. 4.1–17, but it is now enriched by new themes; only from 4.18 onwards are we told about Moses' return to

Egypt. The local scenery, the thorn bush beyond the accustomed grazing area, is confined to 3.1–5. Everything else is speech, for the most part an amplified dialogue between Moses and the deity. This already shows on the purely formal level that the account's stress does not lie on the description of a historical course of events, but on its deeper motivation. The usual division of sources is so confused that it sees vv. 1–5 as a Yahwist component, expanded through vv. 7f.; vv. 16–22 are also largely ascribed to J, although here it is not possible to make a strict and undoubted division of sources, because of the new motifs. Verses 1bβ, 4b, 6, and 9–15 are largely made over to the later Elohist. With this, the important question about the name of the deity also falls to his share. For the analysis see, as well as older commentaries, the following more recent books especially: Noth, *Exodus*, pp. 38ff.; Fohrer, *Überlieferung und Geschichte*, pp. 24ff.; Schmid, *Mose*, pp. 27ff. On the formal structure of the account of the divine call, see Habel, 'Form and Significance', pp. 297ff.; Kutsch, 'Gideons Berufung', pp. 89f.

2. Ex. 3.14.

3. The following studies may be mentioned: Quell, 'Gottesname'; Murtonen, *Philological and Literary Treatise*, pp. 43ff.; Goitein, 'YHWH the Passionate'; Maclaurin, 'YHWH the Origin'; Herrmann, 'Der alttestamentliche Gottesname'; Köhler, 'Vom hebräischen Lexikon', pp. 153f., and KBL pp. 386f.; von Soden, 'Jahwe'.

4. See details in the studies mentioned in the previous note; most recently especially von Soden, op. cit.; see also Noth, *Personennamen*, pp. 111f.

5. Alt, 'Ägyptisches Gegenstück'. The context of the passage from the *Instruction for Merikare*, ll. 94f., was already given in ch. II above. The Egyptian wording runs *wn(n)y wn.kwy*; it therefore uses two different forms of the verb 'to be' (*wnn*), and can consequently be paraphrased as 'I am in that I am the irrevocably existing one'. The second form, an Egyptian pseudo-participle (*wn.kwy*), expresses the enduring quality of a state of affairs and can therefore distinguish the present being (*wnn.y*), the Now, from a completed but always present potentiality of being (*wn.kwy*). In Hebrew, on the other hand, the so-called 'paronomastic relative clause' *'ehyeh 'ašer 'ehyeh* does not offer this possibility of differentiating by changing the tense.

6. Alt, op. cit., col. 160.

7. Von Rad, *Theology* I, p. 182, n. 16 actually talks about a 'grandiloquent formula'.

8. Von Rad, op. cit., p. 182, says that in giving the information which he does Yahweh 'reserves his freedom, a freedom which will be displayed precisely in his being there, in his efficacious presence'. Vriezen has pointed particularly to Yahweh's efficaciously present existence in connection with Ex. 3.14 (*Bertholet-Festschrift*, pp. 498ff. esp. p. 508). Von Soden, op. cit., p. 185, interprets the Tetragrammaton as a name of thanksgiving and gives it the meaning 'He constantly shows himself as helper'. See now also Wolff, 'Jahwe und die Götter', pp. 398ff.; he finds in the self-declaration of Ex. 3.14 the assurance – which is appropriate in every respect – 'I show myself as the one who sets about the work'. Wolff consequently talks about Yahweh as 'the incomparably efficacious one'.

9. To enumerate them in detail: the transformation of water into blood;

frogs; gnats; flies; cattle plague; ulcers; hail; locusts; and darkness.

10. Noth, *Exodus*, pp. 67f.

11. Deut. 4.34; 6.22; 7.9; Ps. 105.27; 135.9; and frequently elsewhere.

12. Ex. 8.18f.; 9.4, 26.

13. The 'destroyer' or 'strangler' is only mentioned once, Ex. 12.23, and is probably an old element surviving from the ideology behind the custom of the passover sacrifice. Incidentally, according to the present account it is clearly Yahweh himself who slays the firstborn. See Noth, *Exodus*, p.91.

14. Pedersen's article, 'Passahfest und Passahlegende', is fundamental. His thesis was taken over in restricted form by Noth (*Überlieferungsgeschichte*, pp. 70ff.). See also Rost, 'Weidewechsel'. For a summing up of more modern literature as well as their own views see Kraus, *Worship in Israel*, pp.45ff.; Fohrer, *Überlieferung und Geschichte*, pp.79ff.; Schmid, *Mose*, pp.43ff.

15. In spite of this, the analysis is still disputed in detail, and especially the allotment of the traditional elements to the source writings. Noth's analysis in *Exodus*, pp. 104ff., gives a more or less rounded impression: he assigns portions to the three source writings, J. E and P, and his conclusions are accepted in the account that follows. Fohrer (*Überlieferung und Geschichte*, pp. 97ff.) takes a different view, excluding P and finding (apart from some additions) only J, E and N, the source he himself pleads for. Von Rabenau's analysis in 'Schilfmeerwunder' only takes account of J and P. At all events, the evidence of the differing motifs and tendencies remains important enough; their assignment to greater complexes, with the aim of finding in each case independent, self-contained narratives of the happenings at the Reed Sea, is a secondary problem which probably cannot be completely clarified.

16. When this thesis is adopted it is generally presupposed that the mountain of God lay beyond the Gulf of Aqaba, i.e., not in the Sinai peninsula but in the north-western part of the Arabian peninsula. The frequently discussed problem of the geographical position of the mountain of God must be left on one side here.

17. On a little hill near what is today *maḥammadīye* and the *ṣabḥat el-bardawīl* (Lake Sirbonis). Eissfeldt, *Baal Zaphon*, pp. 39f.

18. Gardiner, 'Ancient Military Road', pp. 99ff.; Peet, *Egypt*, pp. 141ff.

19. Eissfeldt, *Baal Zaphon*.

20. Quoted from the Loeb edition, vol. I, pp. 99f.

21. *Geographica* XVI, 758; Loeb edition, vol. VII, pp. 273f.

22. *Geographica* I, 58; Loeb edition, vol. I, p. 217.

23. Noth, 'Schauplatz des Meereswunders'.

24. Noth's arguments (op. cit.) are not designed basically to deny the historical possibility that the events may have taken place at Lake Sirbonis; but, for reasons connected with the history of the tradition, he is not prepared to exclude other lakes in the eastern delta region either. Because of the other mentions of the 'Reed Sea' in the Old Testament, Noth is certain that the Gulf of Aqaba is meant; he interprets this as being another attempt at localization from the perspective of a later editing of the tradition. For the historical evaluation of the events, however, the Gulf of Aqaba is practically out of the question. This view is shared by Fohrer, *Überlieferung und Geschichte*, pp. 105f., and Schmid, *Mose*, pp. 53 and 107.

25. For the differing judgments about the Reed Sea motif in the history of the tradition see McCarthy, 'Plagues'; Mowinckel, *Passahlegende*; Coats, 'Reed Sea Motif'.

VI

1. Noth, *Überlieferungsgeschichte*, pp. 5 off., which also lists the many relevant passages. The exodus from Egypt comes out especially clearly at the beginning of the concise summary of fundamental historical events as being God's really main act: Deut. 26.8; 6.21–23; Josh. 24.6, 7. These Old Testament summaries give an outline of salvation history in the narrowest space in the style of a brief historical creed. See here the basic discussion in von Rad, 'The Form-critical Problem', pp. 3ff.

2. On the later history of the exodus traditions in the Old Testament see von Rad, *Theology* I, pp. 187ff.; Rohland, *Erwählungstraditionen*, pp. 24ff.; Lubsczyk, *Auszug*; Herrmann, *Heilserwartungen*, pp. 64ff. and passim.

BIBLIOGRAPHY

Albright, W. F., 'Abram the Hebrew. A New Archaeological Interpretation', BASOR 163, 1961, pp. 36–54.
— 'The Biblical Period, From Abraham to Ezra', in: L. Finkelstein (ed.), *The Jews, Their History and Culture*, 1963.
Alt, A., *Kleine Schriften zur Geschichte des Volkes Israel*, I–III, Munich 1953–59; partial ET, *Essays on Old Testament History and Religion*, Oxford 1966. (The two essays from the *Kleine Schriften* listed below are not translated into English.)
— *Die Herkunft der Hyksos in neuer Sicht*, 1954 = KS III, pp. 72–98.
— *Die Deltaresidenz der Ramessiden*, 1954 = KS III, pp. 176–85.
— 'Ein ägyptisches Gegenstück zu Ex. 3.14', ZAW 58, 1940–41, pp. 159f.
Auerbach, E., *Moses*, Amsterdam 1953.
— *Wüste und Gelobtes Land I. Geschichte Israels von den Anfängen bis zum Tode Salomos*, Berlin 1932.
Bardtke, H., *Vom Nildelta zum Sinai. Bilder zur Landes- und Altertumskunde nach eigenen Aufnahmen des Verfassers während einer Studienreise im Sommer 1966*, Berlin 1968.
Bauer, T., *Die Ostkanaanäer. Eine philologisch-historische Untersuchung über die Wanderschicht der sogenannten 'Amoriter' in Babylonien*, Leipzig 1926.
Von Beckerath, J., *Tanis und Theben*, Ägyptologische Forschungen 16, Glückstadt 1951.
— 'Die Reihenfolge der letzten Könige der 19. Dynastie', ZDMG 106, 1956, pp. 241–51.
— *Untersuchungen zur politischen Geschichte der Zweiten Zwischenzeit in Ägypten*, Ägyptologische Forschungen 23, Glückstadt 1964.

Beer, G. and Galling, K., *Exodus*, HAT I, 3, Tübingen 1939.

Beyerlin, W., *The Origins and History of the Oldest Sinaitic Traditions*, Oxford 1965.

Bonnet, H., *Reallexikon der ägyptischen Religionsgeschichte*, Berlin 1952.

Bottéro, J., *Le Problème des Habiru à la 4e Rencontre Assyriologique Internationale*, Paris 1954.

Bright, John, *A History of Israel*, revd ed., London and Philadelphia 1972.

Caminos, R. A., *Late-Egyptian Miscellanies*, London 1954.

Carter, H., and Mace, A. C., *The Tomb of Tut-Ankh-Amen*, three vols., London 1923–33.

Cazelles, H., 'Patriarches', in: *Supplément au Dictionnaire de la Bible* VII, Paris 1961, pp. 82–156.

— 'Pentateuque', in: *Supplément au Dictionnaire de la Bible* VII, Paris 1964, pp. 708–858.

— 'Les localisations de l'Exode et la critique littéraire', RB 62, 1955, pp. 321–64.

— 'Moses im Licht der Geschichte', in: *Moses in Schrift und Überlieferung*, Düsseldorf 1963, pp. 11–30.

Černý, J., 'Papyrus Salt 124 (Brit. Mus. 10055). With Plates XLII–XLVI', JEA 15, 1929, pp. 243–58.

Coats, G. W., 'The Traditio-historical Character of the Reed Sea Motif', VT 17, 1967, pp. 253–65.

Cornelius, F., 'Mose urkundlich', ZAW 78, 1966, pp. 75–8.

Dictionnaire de la Bible, Supplément, see Cazelles, H.

Die Altorientalische Reiche, see Fischer, *Weltgeschichte.*

Donner, H., 'Adoption oder Legitimation? Erwägungen zur Adoption im Alten Testament auf dem Hintergrund der altorientalischen Rechte', *Oriens Antiquus* 8, 1969, pp. 87–119.

Driver, G. R., 'The Original Form of the Name "Yahweh"; Evidence and Conclusions', ZAW 46, 1928, pp. 7–25.

Dupont-Sommer, A., *Les Araméens*, L'Orient Ancien Illustré 2, Paris 1949.

— 'Sur les débuts de l'histoire araméenne', SVT 1, 1953, pp. 40–9.

Ebeling, E., and Meissner, B., *Reallexikon der Assyriologie*, Berlin 1928ff.

Edel, E., 'Neue keilschriftliche Umschreibungen ägyptischer Namen aus den Boğazköytexten', JNES 7, 1948, pp. 11–24.

Edzard, D. O., *Die Zweite Zwischenzeit Babyloniens*, Wiesbaden 1957.

Eissfeldt, O., *Baal Zaphon, Zeus Kasios und der Durchzug der Israeliten durchs Meer*, Halle 1932.

— 'Palestine in the Time of the Nineteenth Dynasty (a) The Exodus and the Wanderings', CAH 2, 26a, 1965.

— *Die Komposition der Sinai-Erzählung Exodus 19–34*, Sitzungsberichte der Sächsischen Akademie der Wissenschaften zu Leipzig, Phil.-hist. Kl. Bd. 113, Vol. 1, Berlin 1966.

Fischer, *Weltgeschichte 2: Die Altorientalischen Reiche I Vom Paläolithikum bis zur Mitte der 2. Jahrtausends*, 1965;*3 : Die Altorientalischen Reiche II Das Ende des 2. Jahrtausends*, 1966.

Fohrer, G., *Überlieferung und Geschichte des Exodus. Eine Analyse von Ex. 1–15*, BZAW 91, Berlin 1964.

— 'Altes Testament – "Amphiktyonie" und "Bund"?', ThLZ 91, 1966, cols. 801–16; 893–904.

Galling, K., *Die Erwählungstraditionen Israels*, BZAW 48, Giessen 1928.

— *Textbuch zur Geschichte Israels*, Tübingen ²1968.

Gardiner, A. H., 'The Delta Residence of the Ramessides', JEA 5, 1918, pp. 127–38; 179–200; 242–71.

— 'The Ancient Military Road between Egypt and Palestine', JEA 6, 1920, pp. 99–116.

— 'The Geography of the Exodus: An Answer to Professor Naville and Others', JEA 10, 1924, pp. 87–96.

— 'Tanis and Pi-Ramesse: a Retraction', JEA 19, 1933, pp. 122–8.

— *Late-Egyptian Miscellanies*, Bibliotheca Aegyptiaca 7, Brussels 1937.

— *Ancient Egyptian Onomastica*, I, II, Oxford 1947, and volume of illustrations.

Gelin, A., 'Moses im Alten Testament', in: *Moses in Schrift und Überlieferung*, Düsseldorf 1963, pp. 31–57.

Gese, H., 'Bemerkungen zur Sinaitradition', ZAW 79, 1967, pp. 137–54.

Goitein, S. D., 'YHWH the Passionate. The Monotheistic Meaning and Origin of the Name YHWH', VT 6, 1956, pp. 1–9.

Gordon, C. H., *The World of the Old Testament*, London 1960.

Greenberg, M., *The Hab/piru*, AOS 39, New Haven 1955.

Gressmann, H., *Mose und seine Zeit. Ein Kommentar zu den Mose-Sagen*, Göttingen 1913.

— (ed.), *Altorientalische Texte zum Alten Testament*, Berlin and Leipzig ²1926.

— (ed.), *Altorientalische Bilder zum Alten Testament*, Berlin and Leipzig ²1927.

Griffiths, J. W., 'The Egyptian Derivation of the Name Moses', JNES 12, 1953, pp. 225–31.

Gunneweg, A. H. J., *Leviten und Priester*, FRLANT 89, Göttingen 1965.

—'Mose in Midian', ZThK 61, 1964, pp. 1–9.

Habel, N., 'The Form and Significance of the Call Narratives', ZAW 77, 1965, pp. 297–323.

Hamza, M., 'Excavations of the Department of Antiquities at Qantîr (Faqûs District)', ASAE 30, 1930, pp. 31–68.

Hauschild, R., *Über die frühesten Arier im Alten Orient*, Berichte über die Verhandlungen der Sächsischen Akademie der Wissenschaften, Phil.-hist. Klasse, Kl. Bd. 106, vol. 6, Berlin 1962.

Hayes, C. H., *A Papyrus of the Late Middle Kingdom in the Brooklyn Museum (Pap. Brooklyn 35.1446)*, New York 1955.

Helck, W., *Die Beziehungen Ägyptens zu Vorderasien im 3. und 2. Jahrhundert v. Chr.*, Ägyptologische Abhandlungen 5, Wiesbaden 1962.

—'Die Bedrohung Palästinas durch einwandernde Gruppen am Ende der 18. und am Anfang der 19. Dynastie', VT 18, 1968, pp. 472–80.

—'Tkw und die Ramses-Stadt', VT 15, 1965, pp. 35–48.

—'Zur Geschichte der 19. und 20. Dynastie', ZDMG 105, 1955, pp. 27–52.

Helck, W., and Otto, E., *Kleines Wörterbuch der Ägyptologie*, Wiesbaden 1956.

Herrmann, S., *Die prophetische Heilserwartungen im Alten Testament. Ursprung und Gestaltwandel*, BWANT 85, Stuttgart 1965.

— 'Autonome Entwicklungen in den Königreichen Israel und Judah', SVT 17, 1969, pp. 139–58.

— 'Der alttestamentliche Gottesname', EvTh 26, 1966, pp. 281–93.

'Mose', EvTh 28, 1968, pp. 301–28.

— 'Joseph in Ägypten. Ein Wort zu J. Vergotes Buch "Joseph en Égypte"', ThLZ 85, 1960, cols. 827–30.

— 'Der Name JHW₃ in den Inschriften von Soleb. Prinzipielle Erwägungen', *Fourth World Congress of Jewish Studies, Papers*, I, Jerusalem 1967, pp. 213–6.

Hommel, F., *Die altisraelitische Überlieferung in inschriftlicher Beleuchtung*, Munich 1897.

Hornung, E., *Untersuchungen zur Chronologie und Geschichte des Neuen Reiches*, Ägyptologische Abhandlungen 11, Wiesbaden 1964.

James, T. G. H., 'Egypt: From the Expulsion of the Hyksos to Amenophis I', CAH 2.8, 1965.

Janssen, J. M. A., 'Fonctionnaires sémites au service de l'Égypte', *Chronique d'Égypte* 26, no. 51, 1951, 50ff.

— 'A travers les publications égyptologiques récentes concernant l'Ancien Testament; L'Ancient Testament et l'Orient', in *Orientalia et Biblica Lovaniensia*, I, Louvain 1957, pp. 29–63.

— 'Egyptological Remarks on the Story of Joseph in Genesis', in *Jaarbericht no.* 14, *Ex Oriente Lux*, Leiden 1955/56, pp. 63–72.

Jeremias, A., *Das Alte Testament im Lichte des alten Orient*, Leipzig ⁴1930.

Kaiser, O., *Israel und Ägypten: Zeitschrift des Museums zu Hildesheim*, NF 14, Hildesheim 1963.

— *Die mythische Bedeutung des Meeres in Ägypten, Ugarit und Israel*, BZAW 78, Berlin 1959.

— 'Stammesgeschichtliche Hintergründe der Josephsgeschichte', VT 10, 1960, pp. 1–15.

Kees, H., *Ägypten. Kulturgeschichte des Alten Orients* I, Munich 1933.

Keller, C. A., 'Von Stand und Aufgabe der Moseforschung', ThZ 13, 1957, pp. 430–41.

Koch, K., *The Growth of the Biblical Tradition*, London 1969.

— 'Der Tod des Religionsstifters', KuD 8, 1962, 100–23.

— 'Die Hebräer vom Auszug aus Ägypten bis zum Grossreich Davids', VT 19, 1969, pp. 37–81.

Köhler, L., 'Vom hebräischen Lexikon', OTS 8, 1950, pp. 153f.

Kraus, H. J., *Worship in Israel*, Oxford 1966.

Kupper, J.-R., 'Northern Mesopotamia and Syria', CAH 2.1, 1966.

—*Les nomades en Mésopotamie au temps des rois de Mari*, Paris 1957.

Kutsch, E., 'Gideons Berufung und Altarbau Jdc 6.11–24', ThLZ 81, 1956, cols. 75–84.

Langdon, S., and Gardiner, A. H., 'The Treaty of Alliance between Ḫattušili King of the Hittites, and the Pharaoh Ramesses II of Egypt', JEA 6, 1920, pp. 179–205.

Lubsczyk, H., *Der Auszug Israels aus Ägypten. Seine theologische Bedeutung in prophetischer und priestlicher Überlieferung*, Erfurter Theologische Studien 11, Leipzig 1963.

Malamat, A., *Aspects of Tribal Societies in Mari and Israel*, Les

Congrès et Colloques de l'Université de Liège 42, Liège 1967, pp. 129–38.

McCarthy, J., 'Plagues and Sea of Reeds: Exodus 5–14', JBL 85, 1966, pp. 137–58.

Maclaurin, E. C. B., 'YHWH, the Origin of the Tertragrammaton', VT 12, 1962, pp. 439–63.

Meyer, E., *Die Israeliten und ihre Nachbarstämme*, Halle 1906. Reprinted Darmstadt 1967.

— *Geschichte des Altertums* II 1, 2, Darmstadt ³1953.

Meyer, R., *Hebräische Grammatik* I, Berlin ³1966; II, Berlin ³1969.

Möhlenbrink, K., 'Die levitischen Überlieferungen des Alten Testaments', ZAW 52, 1934, pp. 184–231.

Montet, P., *Das alte Ägypten und die Bibel*, Bibel und Archäologie IV, Zurich 1960.

— *Tanis: douze années de fouilles dans une capitale oubliée au Delta égyptien*, 1942.

Morenz, S., *Ägyptische Religion*, Die Religionen der Menschheit 8, Stuttgart 1960.

— *Ägypten und das Berliner Ägyptische Museum* (Museum guide), Berlin 1953.

— *Die Begegnung Europas mit Ägypten. Mit einem Beitrag von Martin Kaiser, Herodots Begegnung mit Ägypten*, Sitzungsberichte der Sächsichen Akademie der Wissenschaften zu Leipzig, Phil.-hist. Kl. Bd. 113, vol. 5, Berlin 1968.

— 'Joseph in Ägypten', ThLZ 84, 1959, cols. 401–16.

— *Die Zauberflöte. Eine Studie zum Lebenszusammenhang Ägypten – Antike – Abendland*, Münstersche Forschungen 5, Münster/ Cologne 1952.

Moscati, S., *Geschichte und Kultur der semitischen Völker*, Zürich/ Cologne 1961; German translation of *Storia e civiltà dei Semiti*.

— 'The Aramaean Ahlamu', JSS 4, 1959, pp. 303–7.

— *The Semites in Ancient History*, Cardiff 1959.

Moses in Schrift und Überlieferung, original title: Cazelles, H. and Gelin, A., *Moise, l'Homme de l'Alliance*, Tournai 1955.

Mowinckel, S., 'Die vermeintliche "Passahlegende". Ex. 1–15 in Bezug auf die Frage: Literarkritik und Traditionskritik', *Studia Theologica* 5, 1951.

Müller, W. M., *Asien und Europa*, Leipzig 1893.

Murtonen, A., *A Philological and Literary Treatise on the Old Testament Divine Names*, Helsinki 1952.

Naville, E., 'The Geography of the Exodus', JEA 10, 1924, pp. 18–39.

Noth, Martin, *History of Israel*, London ²1960.

— *The Old Testament World*, London 1966.

— *Die israelitischen Personennamen im Rahmen der gemeinsemitischen Namengebung*, BWANT 3, 10, Stuttgart 1928, reprinted Hildesheim 1966.

— *Das System der zwolf Stämme Israels*, BWANT 4.1, Stuttgart 1930.

— *Überlieferungsgeschichte des Pentateuch*, Stuttgart 1948, ³1966.

— 'Der Schauplatz des Meereswunders', in *Festschrift Otto Eissfeldt zum 60. Geburtstag*, Halle 1947, pp. 181–90.

— *Exodus*, Old Testament Library, London 1962.

— 'Mari und Israel. Eine Personennamenstudie', in *Geschichte und Altes Testament* (Alt Festschrift), Beiträge zur historischen Theologie 16, Tübingen 1953, pp. 127–52.

— *Die Ursprünge des alten Israel im Lichte neuer Quellen*, Arbeitsgemeinschaft für Forschung des Landes Nordrhein-Westfalen, vol. 94, Cologne and Opladen 1961.

— *Gesammelte Studien zum Alten Testament*, Munich ³1966.

— 'Die Wege der Pharaonenheere in Palästina und Syrien. Untersuchungen zu den hieroglyphischen Listen palästinischer und syrischer Städte', ZDPV 60, 1937, pp. 183ff.; 61, 1938, pp. 26ff.; 277ff.; 64, 1941, 39ff.

Osswald, E., *Das Bild des Mose in der kritischen alttestamentlichen Wissenschaft seit Julius Wellhausen*, Theologische Arbeiten 18, Berlin 1962.

Parrot, A., *Abraham et son temps*, Cahiers d'archéologie biblique 14, Neuchâtel 1962.

Pedersen, J., 'Passahfest und Passahlegende', ZAW 52, 1934, pp. 161–75.

Peet, J. E. *Egypt and the Old Testament*, Liverpool–London 1924.

Posener, G., 'Les asiatiques en Égypte sous les XIIᵉ et XIIIᵉ dynasties', *Syria* 34, 1957, pp. 145–63.

— *Littérature et politique dans l'Égypte de la XIIᵉ dynastie*, Paris 1956.

Pritchard, J. B., *Ancient Near Eastern Texts relating to the Old Testament*, Princeton ²1955.

— *The Ancient Near East in Pictures relating to the Old Testament*, Princeton 1954.

Quell, G., 'Kyrios', C, TDNT III, pp. 1056–80.

von Rabenau, K., 'Die beiden Erzählungen vom Schilfmeerwunder in Exod. 13.17–14.31', in: P. Wätzel and G. Schille (eds.), *Theologische Versuche*, Berlin 1966.

von Rad, G., *Old Testament Theology*, Edinburgh and London, vol. 1, 1962; vol. 2, 1965.

— *The Problem of the Hexateuch and Other Essays*, London 1966.

— *Die Josephsgeschichte*, Biblische Studien 5, Neukirchen ⁴1964.

— *Biblische Josephserzählung und Josephroman*, Munich 1965.

Ranke, H., *Die ägyptische Personennamen*, I, II, Glückstadt 1935.

Redford, D. B., 'Exodus I 11', VT 13, 1963, pp. 401–18.

Reicke, B., and Rost, L. (eds.), *Biblisch-Historisches Handwörterbuch*, I–III, Göttingen 1962–66.

Rohland, E., *Die Bedeutung der Erwählungstraditionen Israels für die Eschatologie der alttestamentlichen Propheten*, Heidelberg 1956.

Rost, L., 'Weidewechsel und altisraelitischer Festkalender', ZDPV, 1943, reprinted in *Das kleine Credo und andere Studien zum Alten Testament*, Heidelberg 1965, pp. 101–12.

Rowley, H. H., *From Joseph to Joshua. Biblical Traditions in the Light of Archaeology*, London 1950.

Schäfer, H., *Amarna in Religion und Kunst*, Leipzig 1931.

Scharff, A., *Der historische Abschnitt der Lehre für Konig Merikare*, Sitzungsberichte der Bayer. Ak. d. Wiss., Phil.-hist. Abt. 1936, vol. 8, Munich 1936.

Scharff, A. and Moortgat, A., *Ägypten und Vorderasien im Altertum*, Munich 1950.

Schmid, H., *Mose. Überlieferung und Geschichte*, BZAW 110, Berlin 1968.

Schmökel, H., *Geschichte des alten Vorderasien*, Handbuch der Orientalistik 2, 3, Leiden 1957.

Schnutenhaus, F., *Die Enstehung der Mosetraditionen*, typescript dissertation, Heidelberg 1958.

Schunck, K. D., *Benjamin. Untersuchungen zur Entstehung und Geschichte eines israelitischen Stammes*, BZAW 86, Berlin 1963.

Seebass, H., *Mose und Aaron, Sinai und Gottesberg*, Diss. Bonn 1962.

— *Der Erzvater Israel und die Einfuhrung der Jahweverehrung in Kanaan*, BZAW 98, Berlin 1966.

Van Seters, J., *The Hyksos. A New Investigation*, New Haven and London 1966.

Simons, J., *Handbook for the Study of Egyptian Topographical Lists relating to Western Asia*, Leiden 1937.

Smend, R., *Das Mosebild von Heinrich Ewald bis Martin Noth*,

Beiträge zur Geschichte der biblischen Exegese 3, Tübingen 1959.

— *Jahwekrieg und Stämmebund. Erwägungen zur ältesten Geschichte Israels*, FRLANT 84, Göttingen 1963.

von Soden, W., *Der Aufstieg des Assyrerreiches als geschichtliches Problem*, AO 37, 1/2, Leipzig 1937.

— 'Jahwe "Er ist, Er erweist sich"', WO III, 1964–66, pp. 177–87.

Spiegelberg, W., *Der Aufenthalt Israels in Ägypten im Lichte der ägyptischen Monumente*, Strassburg ²1904.

Täubler, E., *Biblische Studien. Die Epoche der Richter*, Tübingen 1958.

de Vaux, R., *Die hebräischen Patriarchen und die modernen Entdeckungen*, Düsseldorf 1961, translated from RB 53, 1946, pp. 321–48; RB 55, 1948, pp. 321–47; RB 56, 1949, pp. 5–36 (references here are to the original).

— 'Les patriarches hébreux et l'histoire', RB 72, 1965, pp. 5–28.

Vergote, J., *Joseph en Égypte. Genèse ch. 37–50 à la lumière des études égyptologiques récentes*, Louvain 1959.

Volten, A., *Zwei altägyptische politische Schriften*, Analecta Aegyptiaca IV, Copenhagen 1945.

Vriezen, T. C., 'Ehje ašer ehje': *Festschrift für A. Bertholet*, Tübingen 1950, pp. 498ff.

Weidmann, H., *Die Patriarchen und ihre Religion im Licht der Forschung seit Julius Wellhausen*, FRLANT 94, Göttingen 1968.

Weippert, M., *The Settlement of the Israelite Tribes in Palestine*, SBT II 21, London 1971.

Wolff, H. W., 'Jahwe und die Götter in der alttestamentlichen Prophetie', EvTh 29, 1969, pp. 397–416.

Zobel, H.-J., *Stammesspruch und Geschichte. Die Angaben der Stammessprüche von Gen. 49, Dtn. 33 und Jdc. 5 über die politischen und kultischen Zustände im damaligen 'Israel'*, BZAW 95, Berlin 1965.

INDEX OF MODERN AUTHORS

INDEX OF NAMES AND SUBJECTS

INDEX OF BIBLICAL REFERENCES